Theaters and Their Seating in Japan

Architectural gems from 1911 to 2018

BOOKEND

The Show Will Soon Begin

Ikeda Satoru

What we behold on making our way to and into a theater or concert hall is a sea of audience seating and, beyond, the stage. The view varies greatly by theater and by concert hall. Especially striking is the diversity of the stages. Shaping a unique personality for each are such elements as the sometimes elaborate main curtain, the oftentimes unique configuration of the massive removable orchestra shell, and, on occasion, the imposing presence of a stately pipe organ.

Theaters and concert halls equipped with large stages also have large seating capacities. Architects seek to position all the seats, though, as close as possible to the stage. The history of optimizing theater layouts dates at least from amphitheaters of ancient Greece. Those theaters were bowl-shaped affairs that generally occupied sites on gently sloping land. They wrapped semicircular seating around the "orchestra," a circular space for the chorus in front of the stage. That design minimized the distance between the seating and the stage and maximized visibility and audibility for the audience. It has remained a template for performance hall design to this day.

A performance hall comprises a stage, audience seating, and spaces and equipment for supporting the performance and appreciation functions. The stage needs to be of optimal shape, size, and functionality for its primary purpose, such as theatrical productions or musical performances. Similarly, the audience seating needs to offer maximal visibility and audibility for enjoying performances.

Yet another parameter of performance hall construction is the sense of proximity and solidarity engendered between the audience and the performers and among the members of the audience. An atmosphere of collective intimacy and shared focus amplifies the energy imparted by the performance on stage. Conversely, the absence of such an atmosphere diminishes the power of the performance.

The relative positioning of the stage and the audience seating is thus an important consideration in designing performance halls. Yet the stage has been the primary concern in recent years and the audience seating a secondary concern for architects and other specialists. Their chief concern in regard to audience seating has been with ensuring that it does not interfere with the performances. A maximally fulfilling experience of a performance art depends, however, on a more equal balance between the audience seating and the stage. Both seating and stage have important roles to play in conveying the performance to the eyes and ears of the audience and in relaying the response of the audience to the performers.

That safety and peace of mind for all in the hall are paramount goes without saying. The seating, meanwhile, should be reassuring, as well as comfortable and functional. But more is at stake here.

Enable the audience to become completely and unconsciously absorbed in the performance. That is an important objective in creating a performance hall. Fuel the air of anticipation as the show is about to begin and make the most of the experience for all once it is under way. Thus does the hall transport its audience out of the world of the ordinary for the duration of the performance.

On the following pages are numerous examples of halls in Japan that serve the performing arts in diverse ways. Enjoy this overview of the state of the art in performance halls and in audience seating.

Director and executive adviser
Nagata Acoustics Inc.

Theaters and Their Seating in Japan

Architectural gems from 1911 to 2018

This book was published in 2020 by Bookend Publishing Co., Ltd.,
in conjunction with the Kotobuki Seating 100th Anniversary Project.

Book Design by Shigeru Orihara
Printing and binding by Nissha Printing Communications, Inc.
ISBN978-4-907083-63-2

Japan's Postwar Theaters and Lighting Equipment

Yoshii Sumio
Stage-lighting professional

Halls that escaped the World War II bombing

This overview of Japan's theaters and concert halls is even more meaningful than the casual reader might suspect from the title. The value of those performance halls to the cultural life of their nation is unimaginable for anyone unfamiliar with postwar Japan.

US B-29s laid waste to Tokyo with carpet bombing. Their incendiary bombs left nothing standing across vast swaths of the city. The US military command was already preparing for the occupation, though, and it deliberately spared buildings needed for postwar administration. Two buildings spared in central Tokyo to house occupation administrators were the Dai-Ichi Mutual Life Insurance Building (now DN Tower 21) and the Meiji Mutual Life Insurance Building (now the Meiji Yasuda Seimei Building).

Several theaters also survived the bombing, including the Tokyo Takarazuka Theater (1934–1997), the Marunouchi Shochiku (1924–1984), the original Imperial Theatre (1911–1965, pp. 28–31), and the Yurakuza (1935–1984). They were of limited accessibility to Japanese, however, on account of requisitioning by the occupation authorities. The Tokyo Takarazuka Theater, as the Ernie Pyle Theater, served occupation personnel and their dependents with live musical entertainment. Just a few blocks away, the Marunouchi Shochiku, as the Piccadilly Theater, staged contemporary theatrical productions for occupation audiences.

The Tokyo Takarazuka Theater was among a handful of Japanese performance halls equipped with an orchestra pit and world-class theatrical fixtures. Especially notable was its lighting system. It employed an innovative array of transformers remotely operated with levers and wires. The transformers controlled actuator motors that moved dimmers across multiple presets.

Until the advent of thyristor control in the 1960s, transformer control was a core lighting technology for Japanese performance halls. The transformers, largely iron, were bulky and weighty and required installation near the stage. And the dimmer room needed to be near enough to the transformers for lever-and-wire operation to be feasible. That meant installing it in a wing or in the front lighting room, neither of which offered a good view of the stage.

Preceding transformer control was rheostat control. A showcase of rheostat control was the original Imperial Theatre, a classic European-style venue for opera and ballet productions. The theater featured an inclined stage that rose toward the back. Its wire-operated rheostat dimmers were from Germany's Siemens, and the mechanisms were of sublime manufacture. The newly formed Tokyo Ballet performed *Swan Lake* as its debut production at the Imperial Theatre in August 1946.

Shimada Hiroshi, a ballet dancer, director, and choreographer, spearheaded the establishment of the Tokyo Ballet, which was active until 1950 (and had no direct lineage to the ballet company of the same name that was established in 1964 and that is still active). I cherish memories of its *Swan Lake*, which sparkled like a jewel on the still war-scarred cityscape of the Japanese capital.

The Yurakuza also featured an inclined stage and accommodated 900 people. Its lighting system, of Japanese manufacture, used transformer control with short wires to operate the dimmers remotely. The Komaki Ballet staged the first Japanese performances of *Petrouchka* at the Yurakuza in 1950. Komaki Masahide had directed the aforementioned Tokyo Ballet production of *Swan Lake* in 1946 and had gone on to establish his own ballet company the next year. Before staging the 1950 production of *Petrouchka*, the Komaki Ballet staged *The Nutcracker* at the Nissay Theatre in 1947 and *Prince Igor* at the original Imperial Theatre in 1948. I was on hand for the company's *Petrouchka* and recall well how Stravinsky's breathtaking score was hugely uplifting for those of us who experienced it in Tokyo.

Toho, Japan's dominant theatrical and movie production company, owned the Imperial Theatre and the Yurakuza. Those were the only performance halls open to Japanese that were equipped to properly accommodate opera and ballet productions. Toho eventually withdrew, however, from orchestral, operatic, and ballet productions. That left those of us who staged opera and ballet productions in early-postwar Tokyo with the Tokyo Metropolitan Hibiya Public Hall as our only venue. The Tokyo Metropolitan Hibiya Public Hall, too, had earned a reprieve from the wartime bombing to render service in the occupation as necessary. It seated more than 2,000 people on four levels but was anything but a performance hall. The hall lacked even an orchestra pit, and its acoustics were deplorable.

Dedicated performance halls of the 1960s

Tokyo Bunka Kaikan (pp. 20–27) opened in 1961 as Japan's first performance venue expressly for opera and ballet productions. Its orchestra pit is more than up to the task, and the Main Hall accompanies a proscenium-arch configuration with superb acoustics. Also of note is its flying bridge for illumination, the first of its kind in Japan. All in all, this hall was the finest venue imaginable for its expressed purpose when it was built.

One shortcoming of Tokyo Bunka Kaikan was the transformer control for the lighting system. That meant positioning the dimmer room behind the lower lighting room. The 2014 remodeling included switching to thyristor control for the lighting system, and that allowed for moving the dimmer room to a central position behind the second-level seating.

A Japanese pioneer in thyristor control for performance hall lighting was the Nissay Theatre (pp. 42–45). That venue opened in 1963 with a production of Beethoven's *Fidelio* by the Deutsche Oper Berlin. Its dimmer room occupies a central position at the rear of the seating, which commands a good view of the stage. Exercising voltage control by tugging on wires gave way to phase control at low voltage. Instead of pushing and pulling on hard-to-move levers, the operators could adjust the lighting simply by sliding fader switches among the presets. Those switches and their presets have since given way in the evolution of lighting systems to computerized remote control.

Mingling among my memories of highlights in the evolution of Japan's performance hall lighting are anecdotes of seating. I remember, for example, seeing the architect Murano Togo at the construction site for the Nissay Theatre. That performance hall would incorporate state-of-the-art lighting technology, but Murano was equally interested in the seating. He had the construction team place a full-scale model of a seat in his on-site office. I remember seeing him get in and out of the seat repeatedly, checking the proportions, the contours, and the color and texture of the fabric.

The Nissay Theatre under construction (*left*) and the newly opened Nissay Hibiya Building and the Hibiya streetscape in 1963 (photos courtesy of Nissay Theatre)

How Japan's Performance Halls Have Evolved with the Times

Ito Masaji
President
Theatre Workshop Co., Ltd.

Halls that do justice to the performing arts

Background   Japan accumulates a diversity of performance halls in the first half of the 20th century but turns its attention in the early postwar years to building multipurpose public halls that accommodate large audiences. Attention shifts in the 1960s to building performance halls that do justice to classical music, theater, and dance.

Ginza Saison Theatre—a place and seating for drama

The new emphasis on doing justice in architecture to specific performance genres culminated in the Ginza Saison Theatre. Tsutsumi Seiji, the charismatic and culturally attuned leader of the Saison retailing conglomerate (Seibu department stores, Seiyu supermarkets, Family Mart convenience stores, Muji lifestyle shops), opened that theater in 1987. It was the venue for several highly regarded theatrical productions as the Ginza Saison Theatre and, after a corporate restructuring in 2000, as Le Theatre Ginza by Parco. The theater closed in 2013.

Kikutake Kiyonori, Ginza Saison Theatre's architect, secured extensive input from theater professionals, including me, in designing the venue. That input shaped even such details as the wooden armrests on the seats and the 100% natural fabric of the seat upholstery. Kikutake related an interesting aspect of how theater seating differed from concert hall seating based on his consultants' advice.

Musical appreciation, observed Kikutake, is largely a two-way dynamic between the performers and each listener. Concert hall seating therefore needs to be wide enough that the concertgoers are unconcerned with the individuals on their left and right. On the other hand, appreciating theatrical performances entails more of a shared response by the members of the audience. Playhouse seating thus needs to be narrow enough to encourage awareness of fellow theatergoers. Thus were the seats in the Ginza Saison Theatre, at 49 centimeters across, 3 centimeters narrower than those in Suntory Hall, a classical music venue built at around the same time. Yet I have no memory of anyone ever complaining that the Ginza Saison Theatre seating felt cramped. Participating in the Ginza Saison Theatre project was an epiphany for me in regard to the importance of seating in performance hall architecture.

Tokyo Bunka Kaikan—hexagonal geometry for total visibility

The theatrical director Oguri Tetsuya has a persistent admonition for architects and others of us responsible for creating performance halls. "No hall built in the decades since Tokyo Bunka Kaikan (pp. 20–27) opened," he emphasizes, "has excelled that venue."

Tokyo Bunka Kaikan opened in 1961 and emerged from a remodeling in 2014. Its Main Hall seats more than 2,300 people yet offers an excellent view of the stage for all. That is a feat that has proved difficult to match at other venues and is due to the hall's hexagonal geometry. Arraying the seating, including the multilevel balcony seating, to face three of the hexagonal stage's facets ensures good visibility for all. From the vantage of the performers, the seating appears to wrap around the stage. Yet the hexagonal configuration eliminates the blind spots that occur with the horseshoe configuration of traditional European opera houses.

Germany, which lost a lot of its opera houses in World War II, became an architecture laboratory for modern opera houses. The marvelously resurrected Semperoper Dresden, for example, replicates the foyer and audience seating of the original in a thoroughly modern context. Performance halls in several cities of the former Federal Republic of Germany (West Germany) feature newly configured audience seating. The rebuilt halls have improved on the horseshoe-shaped configuration of the prewar halls with a sledge-shaped configuration. Their balcony seating employs projected boxes that provide an unobstructed vantage of the stage.

Tokyo Bunka Kaikan's configuration, also seen in the Main Theater at the Aichi Prefectural Art Theater, is an adaptation of the German advance in performance hall architecture. The hexagonal design, however, was an original innovation by the architects, Mayekawa Associates, Architects and Engineers. We marvel, meanwhile, at the bowl-shaped topography of the first-level seating and at how the seating radiates away from the front three facets of the stage's hexagon at varied angles.

Le Theatre Ginza by Parco (formerly the Ginza Saison Theatre)   Photo: Shikano Yasushi

Purpose-specific halls

Background   A recognition that multipurpose halls had proved to be purposeless halls sparks interest in building dedicated, purpose-specific venues. Performing arts complexes include concert halls, opera houses, and experimental theaters. Stage equipment becomes more sophisticated, halls gain motor-driven acoustic panels, and movable prosceniums appear. Classical music is the main purpose for most of the large halls built across the Japanese landscape. The rich resonance of those halls proves unsuitable, however, for theatrical productions and talks, which narrows their applicability more than their builders intended. Later advances in sound systems will restore versatility while honoring the purpose-specific intent.

Suntory Hall—a dedicated venue for classical music

A standout among Japan's first performance venues built especially to accommodate classical music was Suntory Hall (pp. 54–57), opened in 1986 and refurbished in 2017. Suntory Hall's architects, who reportedly drew inspiration from Berlin's Konzerthaus, employed "vineyard-style" surround seating in the Main Hall. The seating is in separate blocks, similar to sections of a vineyard, and each block has a distinct vantage of the stage. Low dividers between the seating blocks serve double duty as acoustic panels.

The division by block complicates the flow of concertgoers in and out of the hall, and the differences in vantage complicate the task of selecting seats. But Suntory Hall's architects have achieved benefits with the sectional layout that more than outweigh the drawbacks.

Fine-tuning the angle of the seats has secured a reliable line of sight for each occupant, and the acoustics are magnificent. On the second level, the handrails in front of the forward-most seats trace an appealing zigzag pattern at the staggered ends of the rows.

Luna Hall—a pioneering experimental theater

Ashiya City built Luna Hall (Ashiya Municipal Grand Hall) in 1970 as an experimental venue for theatrical productions. Although not included in the case studies presented in this volume, that venue warrants attention for its interior, including the seating.

Luna Hall's all-black interior is of adaptable configuration. The stage can be an end stage that faces the audience on a single side. It can be a thrust stage that faces the audience on three sides. Or it can occupy the center of the hall, surrounded completely by the audience.

Yamasaki Yasutaka, Luna Hall's architect, opted for low seat backs. He wanted to heighten the audience members' awareness of each other and therefore wanted each theatergoer to see before her or him not just a seat back but a person. Another advantage of the low seat backs is that even small children have an unobstructed view of the stage.

Saitama Arts Theater—a cluster of purpose-specific halls

The Saitama Arts Theater (pp. 64–69) opened in 1994 with four purpose-built halls, one each for theatrical, musical, dance, and video productions. It has earned a great deal of architectural acclaim, including the prestigious Design Division prize bestowed annually by the Architectural Institute of Japan. Koyama Hisao, the Saitama Arts Theater's architect, has imparted a unique personality to all of the halls.

Each of the three halls for live performances overlaps new and old elements of the performance hall tradition. The Main Theater, for theatrical productions, combines elements of Georgian-era British theaters and late-17th-century Kabuki theaters and reproduces the surprisingly similar sense of scale evoked by each. In the Concert Hall, illumination with high-positioned sidelights is a borrowing from Austria's Musikverein Wien. The stage in the Adaptable Theater, for dance productions, was originally semicircular, on the Greco-Roman model, but the remodeling of the Saitama Arts Theater in 2011 included stretching the circular contour ovally. Linking all three halls for live performances are a circular courtyard and a long, broad galleria.

The Saitama Arts Theater exemplifies the trend toward purpose-specific venues for the performing arts. Two other examples of that trend are the Tokyo Metropolitan Theatre (pp. 70–73) and the Aichi Prefectural Art Theater (pp. 74–75). The Tokyo Metropolitan Theatre comprises the 1,999-seat Concert Hall, the 834-seat Playhouse, and two smaller theaters. A remodeling in 2012 included upgrading the Playhouse's purpose-specific functionality under the oversight of the theatrical director and actor Noda Hideki.

Halls for broad-ranging cultural promotion

Background   Venues supplement performance spaces with rehearsal halls, practice rooms, archival centers, and other facilities for promoting the performing arts on a continuing basis. Meanwhile, the venues assume a role as public halls that transcends the performing arts and encompasses a broadened scope of community activity, including even industrial promotion.

Chino Cultural Complex—from art and culture to industry

The Chino Cultural Complex (pp. 126–131), completed in 2005, has become a model for performance halls in Japan's regional cities. It handles events for promoting local industry, as well as musical, theatrical, and dance productions. The complex incorporates several features for supporting each kind of event as a specialized venue.

Air casters allow for repositioning the banks of seats in the Multi Hall to adapt the layout to different needs, and the stage configuration is also adaptable to different kinds of events. The stage can become a thrust stage, for example, to accommodate Shakespearean works. For fashion shows, the organizers can deploy a runway through the seating. The seating can even surround the stage.

A recent production of a play staged by Chino residents involved reversing the position of the stage and the seating in the Multi Hall. The story was about encounters between Japanese of today and from the prehistoric, Jomon period. In the closing scene, the Jomon Japanese return to their original period. The wall between the foyer and the audience seating is completely removable, and the director made effective use of that feature to dramatize the departure.

As at Ashiya's Luna Hall, the theater adaptability engenders unprecedented interaction between the performers and the audience. It engenders, too, possibilities that transcend the performing arts. The Chino Cultural Complex hosts multifarious events for the citizenry of its host community.

Grassroots mobilization

Background   Community focus elicits increased engagement by residents. The halls attract daily interchange and become platforms for community vitalization.

Sakura Hall, Kitakami City Cultural Center—a platform for daily comings and goings

Performance halls, which once drew people only with scheduled productions, now draw people throughout the week with varied offerings. Witness Sakura Hall, at the Kitakami City Cultural Center. That venue, completed in 2003, is the work of the late architect Noguchi Hideyo, of Kume Sekkei. Its Art Factory comprises 21 rooms for such purposes as holding meetings, engaging in facets of traditional Japanese culture, and rehearsing music.

Sakura Hall has three performance halls, and the Art Factory occupies a central position between the three. The Art Factory's smaller rooms are glass walled, and passersby catch glimpses of such activity as rock bands rehearsing and dancers learning new steps. Chairs and tables dot the wooden deck between the rooms. Some of the occupants of the rehearsal rooms are students from a nearby high school, and some of their fellow students drop by to do homework or to chat on the deck. People of all ages use the Art Factory, occasioning intergenerational communication and understanding.

The Architectural Institute of Japan recognized the contributions of Sakura Hall to promoting community interaction in awarding it a Design Division prize in 2006. Three works earned prizes from the institute that year, the other two being the 21st Century Museum of Contemporary Art, Kanazawa (architecture by SANAA), and the Tomihiro Art Museum, in Gumma Prefecture (architecture by AAT + Yokomizo Architects). The Kanazawa museum also features glass-walled construction and numerous small rooms, but Sakura Hall, completed a year earlier, is the work that became a template for subsequent projects of its kind.

Sakura Hall's influence is visible in a majority of the proposals submitted for performance hall projects for the next several years. The judges for the Architectural Institute of Japan's prize examined the candidate works in winter. What registered more powerfully with them than the snow-covered exteriors, however, was the warmth of the community vitality inside.

Küste (Katsuura City Art and Cultural Exchange Center)
—an arena that doubles as a performance hall

Yasuda Toshiya has handled multiple performance hall projects at the architectural firm Yamashita Sekkei. Two that appear in this volume are Küste (pp. 216–219), which opened in 2014 in Chiba Prefecture, and Namiki Square (pp. 228–231), completed two years later in Fukuoka Prefecture. At Küste, Yasuda created what is essentially an arena that can be converted into a performance hall. He employed rollback chairs, which are easy to move about and easy to stow.

The people of Katsuura, a small city, use Küste mainly as an arena, seating stowed, and infrequently as a performance hall, seating deployed. Performance halls account for a declining share of people's consumption of performance art in the age of YouTube, but designing and managing venues like Küste as inviting hubs of community activity can attract robust and continuing flows of visitors.

Right, upper photo: The building that houses the Kitakami City Cultural Center and Sakura Hall Photo: Ito Masaji
Right, lower photo and above: Sakura Hall's Art Factory Photos: Asakawa Satoshi

Memories of Performance Hall Seats

Kushida Kazuyoshi
Theatrical director

Villagers of old would gather under a large tree just outside their village to hold celebrations and to enjoy the music and other offerings of itinerant entertainers. They would also assemble under the tree on sad occasions to sing and console one another. Together under the tree, the villagers would marvel at the wonders of creation, sometimes laughing at the absurdities of the world.

Seating under the tree was on grass. Thus is the Japanese word for play (as in theatrical performance), *shibai*, a compound of the words for turf (*shiba*) and being [on] (*i*). The venue later gained a roof and walls, and people sat on cushions arrayed on tiered seating to enjoy the stage performance.

The word *gekijo* (playhouse) entered the lexicon as the term for a building where theatrical performances took place. Still, Japanese frequently adhered to the reading *shibai* when they encountered the new compound of the words for play (*geki*) and place (*jo*).

Cushions were presumably more comfortable than grass-covered ground under a tree, but their positioning inside a purpose-built structure was more restrictive. On the grass under the tree, members of the audience could move about at will. They could even roll about on the ground or, if the spirit so moved them, get up and run around.

The tradition of freedom under the tree persisted into the playhouse despite the territorial delineation imposed by the cushions. Some playgoers would assume a reclining posture atop their cushions. Some would react to exemplary performances by tossing their cushions toward the stage, the equivalent of shouting, "Bravo!"

Now, our theaters have row after orderly row of fixed seating. Each seat in a theater is of the same size and feel as the others, seemingly devoid of personality. Yet I always perceive a beauty in the orderly waves of seating at the theater and discover an individuality in my assigned seat. Whispering that individuality to me is the cumulative memory of the thousands of individuals who have thrilled to performances in that hall. Underlying that individuality is the history of people watching plays while lolling on turf under a tree or while sitting on cushions in an early playhouse.

A unique and original coalescence of that history is the seat that welcomes me at the theater. Attuned to the tradition that I inherit on taking my place in the hall, I fairly tremble with anticipation.

Implements of Magic

Naito Hiroshi
Architect

An unpleasant experience in early childhood left me with what is apparently a mild case of claustrophobia. A performance hall is a dark enclosure. Yet people willingly submit themselves to sitting motionless in the cramped and dark environment for hours on end. If an alien were to witness the ever so unnatural scene, he or she would surely find it remarkable.

The 20th-century literary critic Yoshimoto Takaaki memorably coined the phrase "joint illusion." He applied it to such constructs as nations, regions, villages, and families. Yet we can regard performance halls, too, as gestation sites for the joint illusion. In a hall for a couple of hours, people jointly experience a staged performance, be it a play, a musical concert, a ballet, a movie, or whatever. They give themselves over to the performance, sharing in the impressions that it imparts. The hall occupants immerse themselves, that is, in the joint illusion.

People who lead lives largely detached from one another assemble in the performance hall and, during their time together there, share the experience of the performance. Together, they experience the sorrow, the glee, the anger, or whatever emotions the performance induces. That shared experience is what the performance hall renders possible.

No such sharing occurs when watching television or peering at a computer screen alone. Virtual reality technology has made impressive strides, but it is nothing like what people experience in a performance hall. Sharing with strangers in a hall the temporally transcendent phenomenon of a performance is a once-in-a-lifetime encounter, and virtual reality cannot begin to replicate that experience. Thus is performance hall architecture, however unnatural it might be, certain to be with us for the long term. Performance halls are sure to endure, no matter how virtual reality technology might evolve.

We lose ourselves completely to what unfolds on the stage. The experience is something akin to leaving our bodies. We entrust our very selves to the images spun by the play, the music, the dancing, the movie, the what have you. We succumb proactively to the joint illusion, abandoning our corporeal being.

As long as we remain preoccupied with our bodies, we cannot move beyond the confines of our individual identity. Well-made performance hall seats are, in that sense, implements of magic—the magic of losing ourselves to the performance. Those implements enable us to forget that we are shut up in a dark box. They help us disregard our cramped and uncomfortable circumstances there. They disconnect us from awareness of the passage of time. They purge from our minds all thoughts of the world outside.

The seats, as implements of magic, ought to be no more physically substantive than air. Ideally, they ought to do their work of supporting us without possessing physical existence. That is impossible, of course, in the spatial context that we accept and occupy as reality. We should retain, however, our non-corporeal ideal for performance hall seats.

Advances in neuroscience and in physiology are gradually elucidating the mysteries of the mind and of the body. Creators of performance hall seating will incorporate those advances in their implements of magic and thereby better enable audiences to lose themselves to the performance.

The implements of magic will better perform their function as they become less physically imposing. Similarly, theaters and concert halls will better fulfill their function of immersing audiences in performances as their brick-and-mortar aspect fades. That transcendence of physicality will be the essence of the joint illusion in the future of performance arts appreciation. Then will we move a step closer to realizing the real unreality of a long-held ideal for drama, music, dance, and cinema.

A Crucial Prop for the Appreciation of Performing Arts

Kusaka Toshiya
Theater planning consultant

A vinyl sheet stretched over a plot of land. A fraying carpet laid on the sheet. If lucky, some cushions to sit on. The "theater seating" of my early days in drama was hardly opulent. Our theatrical settings gained a new allure with the advent of itinerant troupes that staged performances in tents.

A still-earlier memory of "performance hall" seating is from my days as a junior high school student in Okayama Prefecture. We'd sit on straw mats laid on the wooden floor in the gymnasium and listen, our arms wrapped around our knees, to visiting artists, such as the pianist Iwasaki Shuku and the cellist Tsutsumi Tsuyoshi. I've always blamed the uncomfortable seating for my inability to remember what works we heard there.

Performance hall seating is more than just chairs. Maximizing the capacity of large halls are tiered balconies, which shape the aesthetic experience of the halls, as well as accommodating their occupants. Also shaping the aesthetic experience for the occupants of the chairs in the hall are the colors and contours of the walls and the ceiling. Heightening anticipation of what is about to begin is the dimming of the lighting over and around the seating. All of these and other variables combine with the shape and feel and color of the actual chairs to produce the phenomenon perceived as "seating."

The chairs installed in Japanese performance halls a half century ago were nothing describable even charitably as comfortable. Technological inadequacy might have been part of the problem. A bigger reason, however, was that the audiences and the performers simply didn't expect anything better. That has changed in recent decades, and expectations of performance hall seating have mounted. People now regard venturing out to the theater or to a concert as an opportunity to enjoy time in a stimulating environment, as well as to partake of a play or music. Performance hall seating has two important roles to play in fulfilling that expectation.

One important role of performance hall seating is that of hospitality. The seats must enable their occupants to absorb the performance fully. I remember all too well knees bumping up against seat backs in narrow row spacing, chair seats and backs that were unbearably hard, squeaking that arose at the slightest movement, and ill-conceived reclining mechanisms that made maintaining a comfortable posture for enjoying the performance difficult. Another problem, though not the fault of the chairs, was vertical and horizontal positioning that sometimes impinged on the field of view.

The other important role of performance hall seating is that of fostering solidarity. A collective affinity is central to the enjoyment of the performance for the entire audience. The lateral spacing of the seats should be close enough and the seat backs low enough to engender mutual awareness and a visceral, shared response. The applause should be a unified outpouring of collective exuberance.

Thus is the seating an integral element of the performance hall environment. It needs to mesh organically with the other elements of that environment, and it needs to continue evolving to support new possibilities in performance art appreciation. Let us enjoy those possibilities as extensions of the appeal that we once enjoyed sitting shoulder to shoulder on worn cushions.

Acknowledgement   The publisher expresses gratitude for the generous cooperation of the administrators of the performance halls presented in this book and by the architects responsible for several of the halls.

About This Book
· This book presents 57 performance halls in four chronologically ordered chapters.
· In selecting examples of performance halls for this book, the editors considered such factors as specialized orientation, conceptualization, architectural elements, geographical distribution, and architect. The editors sought additionally to include examples of performance halls that marked a departure in their milieu.
· Accompanying each example is an outline that details the location, the owner(s), the architect(s), the date of completion, the date of a major remodeling (if applicable), and the maximum seating capacity (including fixed seating, movable seating, removable seating, and wheelchair seating space).
· The photographs are primarily from an archive maintained by Kotobuki Seating, though the editors have secured some of the photographs anew from the performance halls and the architects. A list of photo credits appears on page 263.

The Venues in Brief
Location, owner(s); architect(s); date of completion; date of major remodeling (if applicable); maximum seating capacity (including fixed seating, movable seating, removable seating, and wheelchair seating space); and photograph descriptions (including page numbers and, in boxes, reference numbers)
A listing of photo credits appears on page 263.

1

Coming to Terms with the Modern Era

Halls completed from 1911 to 1989

Tokyo Bunka Kaikan

■ Location: Taito Ward, Tokyo ■ Owner: Tokyo Metropolitan Government
■ Architect: Mayekawa Associates, Architects and Engineers ■ Remodeling: Mayekawa Associates, Architects and Engineers
■ Completed: 1961 ■ Remodeled: 2014 ■ Seating: Main Hall, 2,317; Recital Hall, 653

The Tokyo Metropolitan Government commissioned the architect Maekawa Kunio to design Tokyo Bunka Kaikan to help commemorate the city's 500th anniversary. City officials wanted to reinforce Tokyo's cultural foundation with a venue for world-class opera and ballet performances. Tokyo Bunka Kaikan has fulfilled its founding spirit superbly, starting with inaugural-year performances by the Wiener Staatsoper (Vienna State Opera) and continuing annually with visits by leading opera and ballet companies, symphony orchestras, chamber music groups, and solo artists from around the world.

Tokyo Bunka Kaikan has earned acclaim as a masterpiece of postwar modernism in Japanese architecture. In 2003, the Japanese chapter of Docomomo (Documentation and Conservation of buildings, sites and neighborhoods of the Modern Movement) International named Tokyo Bunka Kaikan an exemplar of its namesake movement. Projecting from the walls in the Main Hall (pp. 20–23) are cloud-like wooden objects by the sculptor Mukai Ryokichi. They perform a sound-scattering function that contributes to the hall's superlative acoustics. Scattered through the chiefly red seating are seats upholstered in yellow, blue, or green. The chromatic mix yields a pleasing allusion to a flower garden and makes empty seats stand out less.

In addition to the Main Hall and the Recital Hall (pp. 24–25), Tokyo Bunka Kaikan houses practice rooms, meeting rooms, and a music library. Columns, a starry ceiling, and leaf-patterned flooring in the lobby and foyer (p. 26) harmonize with the building's verdant sylvan setting in Tokyo's Ueno Park. Those elements testify to the influence that Maekawa absorbed from his teacher, Le Corbusier.

The Seating Refurbishment at Tokyo Bunka Kaikan
Egawa Toru Mayekawa Associates, Architects and Engineers

Remodeling Tokyo Bunka Kaikan in 2014 entailed putting in place scaffolding for work on the ceilings in the Main Hall, the Recital Hall, and the lobby and foyer. That meant temporarily removing nearly 3,000 seats and finding a place to store them during the remodeling work.

Tokyo Bunka Kaikan's maintenance records illuminated a solution. We learned that the seating in the Main Hall, which had a high rate of utilization, had undergone refurbishing twice since the building's completion in 1961 and that 15 years had elapsed since the last refurbishment. So our client and we decided to take the opportunity to refurbish the entire complement of seats. That included replacing all of the urethane foam cushioning and fabric covering, repairing the wooden parts as necessary, and repainting the cast-iron legs.

Acoustical engineers advised that replacing the urethane foam would increase sound absorption and affect the hall's acoustics adversely and that the earlier refurbishments had included laminating the inner surface of the fabric covering to minimize the sound absorption. The seats in the Main Hall and in the Recital Hall had undergone refurbishing at different times, and examination of their inner-surface laminate revealed differences in the material and thickness employed.

We therefore began tests to determine the optimal material and thickness of the laminate. Our testing encompassed four patterns: laminate of the same thickness and material last used in the Main Hall seating, no laminate, and laminate of two thicknesses and materials different from that last used in the Main Hall seating. Based on our findings, we selected a laminate of polyvinyl chloride in a thickness favorable to seating comfort.

For the fabric covering, we compared a wool prototype from the supplier and a sample of the wool fabric employed in the 1999 refurbishment. A difference in appearance was readily apparent to the eye. That difference, we determined, was on account of the napping used in both samples. Napping is a standard procedure for enhancing the feel of wool fabric. We had opted, however, for a specially ordered weave of a single-color warp and a two-color woof, and napping resulted in blurring the three colors. So we eschewed napping to achieve a fabric as close as possible to that employed in the most recent refurbishment.

Imperial Theatre

■Location: Chiyoda Ward, Tokyo ■Owner: Toho Co., Ltd. ■Architect: Taniguchi Yoshiro
■Completed: 1966 (original completed in 1911) ■Remodeled: 2018 ■Seating: 1,897

The original Imperial Theatre, financed by a consortium of pioneering industrialists, was Japan's first Western-style theater. Taniguchi Yoshiro created the building that houses the present Imperial Theater on the site of the original in 1966. He was a seminal figure in Japanese architectural modernism. And his Imperial Theatre is an innovative fusion of Western and traditional Japanese influences. Stained glass and sculptural decorations by the noted artist Inokuma Genichiro grace the opulent lobby.

The Imperial Theatre remains synonymous with large-scale musicals and plays. A thorough remodeling in 2018 retained the theater's trademark purple seats while adjusting their positioning to strengthen the sense of connection with the stage.

Osaka City Central Public Hall

■ Location: Osaka City, Osaka ■ Owner: Osaka City
■ Architects: Okada Shinichiro, Tatsuno Kingo, Kataoka Yasushi ■ Remodeling: Asakura Associates
■ Completed: 1918 ■ Remodeled: 2002 ■ Seating: Main Hall, 1,161; Middle-Size Hall, 500; Small Hall, 150

A Japanese financier impressed by the public buildings
he saw in the United States donated funding for what
became the Osaka City Central Public Hall. The three-
story steel frame and brick building reopened in 2002
after three and a half years of refurbishing that upgraded
the lighting, acoustics, and stage equipment and
restored the coved ceilings and chandeliers lost to an
earlier remodeling. The Osaka City Central Public Hall
received a designation from the Japanese government in
that year as an important cultural property. That
designation cited the building for the excellence of its
interior and exterior design, including the arched roof
and the ceiling and wall murals.

Fourteen columns line the periphery of the 810-
seat first floor of the Main Hall, and the 351-seat second
floor wraps around the columns. The seats feature cast-
aluminum legs and distinctively shaped backs that
resonate with the neo-renaissance architecture.

ROHM Theatre Kyoto

- Location: Kyoto City, Kyoto ■ Owner: Kyoto City
- Architect: Mayekawa Associates, Architects and Engineers ■ Remodeling:Kohyama Atelier
- Completed: 1960 ■ Remodeled: 2016 ■ Seating: Main Hall, 2,005; South Hall, 716

What is now ROHM Theatre Kyoto opened in 1960 as the Maekawa Kunio–designed Kyoto Kaikan. The modernist building was an early Japanese example of a multipurpose public hall and was long Kyoto's only theater that accommodated 2,000 people. It became a beloved node of cultural activity in the city.

ROHM Co., Ltd., a Kyoto-based electronic components manufacturer, funded the remodeling of the theater, which reopened as ROHM Theatre Kyoto in 2016. The newly built Main Hall stands on the former site of the Kyoto Kaikan's No. 1 Hall. It retains the 2,000-person, multilevel capacity of its predecessor and offers an expanded stage suitable for ballet and opera.

Koyama Hisao, the architect responsible for the remodeling, adopted the colorful, eccentric touch of the Rimpa school in the interior. In keeping with that choice, the fabric on the seats sports a pampas grass motif.

The former No. 2 Hall was reborn after remodeling as the South Hall, a medium-sized multipurpose venue also equipped with a stage. All of the seats on the ground level, on the second level at the rear of the hall, and in the balconies on either side of the hall offer a sense of immediacy with the performers.

Enriching the experience for concertgoers and theatergoers are a bookstore-café, a restaurant, and a common lobby that stretches between the halls. A spacious plaza is a welcoming interface on the community for ROHM Theatre Kyoto.

41

Nissay Theatre

■ Location: Chiyoda Ward, Tokyo ■ Owner: Nippon Life Insurance Company ■ Architect: Murano Togo
■ Completed: 1963 ■ Remodeled: 2016 ■ Seating: 1,334

The Nissay Theatre resides inside Nippon Life Insurance's headquarters building, which faces Hibiya Park near the Imperial Palace. Installing a full-size theater inside a commercial office building was a revolutionary concept when the architect Murano Togo undertook the commission. The Nissay Hibiya Building became a decisive facet of Murano's incredibly diverse legacy. Highlighting its theater's inaugural-year program was a production of Beethoven's *Fidelio* by the Deutsche Oper Berlin. That set the tone for what would become a tradition of presenting world-class productions.

Murano imparted gravitas to the building by deploying *mannari-ishi* pinkish granite in the exterior. Establishing a mood of anticipation are the red carpeting on the grand staircase and spiral stairway that convey spectators to their seats and the marble tesserae ornamentation in the walls of the lounge on each floor. Engendering an air of fantasy are the curvature of the theater ceiling and walls, the variegated glass tiling on the walls, and the multicolored plaster ceiling embedded with some 20,000 pearl oyster shells. A refurbishing in 2015 and 2016 honored Murano's intent. It included, for example, replacing the fabric on the seats and restoring the original luster of their salmon pink.

National Theatre

■ Location: Chiyoda Ward, Tokyo ■ Owner: Japan Arts Council
■ Architects: Iwamoto Hiroyuki and colleagues at Takenaka Corporation
■ Completed: 1966 ■ Remodeled: 2009 ■ Seating: Large Theatre=1,610/ Small Theatre=590

Japan's government built the National Theatre to stage performances, cultivate artists, and support research in the traditional performance arts. It positioned the theater on the west side of the Imperial Palace, and the architects deployed dark brown concrete in a manner redolent of the interlocking log construction of eighth-century Japanese storehouses. The primary fare in the main theater is Kabuki, and the stage features a rotating platform 20 meters in diameter, 17 lifts of different sizes, and a trap cellar large enough to accommodate hefty equipment. In keeping with the refined tone of the theater, the seating evokes a plush elegance, including fabric across even the back of each seat.

National Noh Theatre

■ Location: Shibuya Ward, Tokyo ■ Owner: Japan Arts Council ■ Architect: Oe Hiroshi Architecture Office
■ Completed: 1983 ■ Remodeled: 2005 ■ Seating: 627

Experiencing Noh drama and its comical Kyogen counterpart properly requires a specially designed stage, and the National Noh Theatre serves as Japan's flagship venue for those performing arts. Its metallic roof emulates the thatched cypress bark of formal Japanese architecture. Inside, the atmosphere is redolent of the real cypress employed in the stage. The length and angle of the *hashigakari* bridgeway are consistent with the specifications of the Noh theaters of old.

Noh drama earned an inscription in 2008 on the UNESCO Representative List of the Intangible Cultural Heritage of Humanity, and the National Noh Theatre attracts an international cast of visitors. Each seat has a personal LCD panel for displaying librettos and summaries in Japanese, English, and, sometimes, other languages.

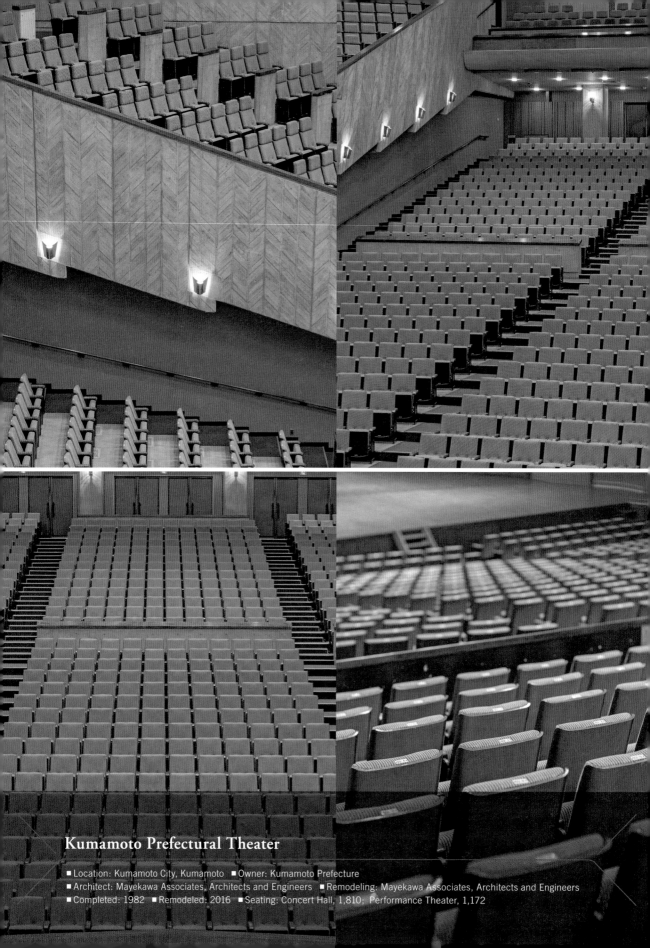

Kumamoto Prefectural Theater

- Location: Kumamoto City, Kumamoto ■ Owner: Kumamoto Prefecture
- Architect: Mayekawa Associates, Architects and Engineers ■ Remodeling: Mayekawa Associates, Architects and Engineers
- Completed: 1982 ■ Remodeled: 2016 ■ Seating: Concert Hall, 1,810; Performance Theater, 1,172

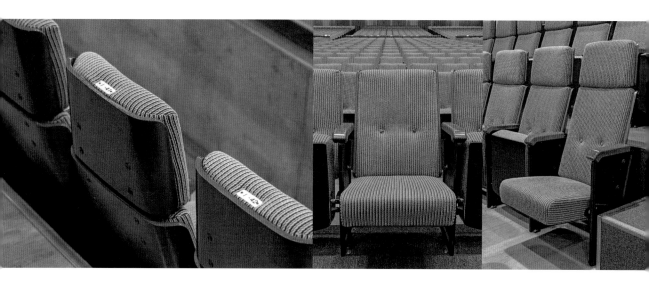

Kumamoto Prefecture turned for its prefectural theater to the designers of Tokyo Bunka Kaikan (pp. 20–27): Mayekawa Associates, Architects and Engineers. That firm responded with a structure that, with its low profile and pale red exterior, is remarkably unimposing for its large capacity. Its architects angled the walls in the Concert Hall to optimize the acoustics and achieved a long, two-second reverberation time. The air-conditioning equipment and other sources of mechanical noise went into the basement to avoid impinging on musical performances.

In the Performance Theater, the second-level seating wraps around the first-level seating below. A steep incline for the third-level seating ensures good visibility, even from the rearmost seats.

Mayekawa Associates chose rounded backs and soft armrests for the seats for the Concert Hall and Performance Theater. The firm's innovative design for the leg linkages has become the standard for theater seating in Japan. The twining motif on the upholstery echoes a traditional Japanese pattern and appears as well on the floor tile laid inside and outside the building.

Suntory Hall

■ Location: Minato Ward, Tokyo   ■ Owner: Suntory Holdings Limited
■ Architects: Yasui Architects and EngineersInc.; Irie Miyake Architects and Engineers
■ Completed: 1986   ■ Remodeled: 2017   ■ Seating: Main Hall, 2,006; Blue Rose (small hall), 432

Tokyo gained its first venue devoted to large-scale classical music concerts with the 1986 opening of Suntory Hall. The hall introduced Japan to "vineyard-style" surround seating, which engages all members of the audience in the performance. Also new with Suntory Hall was the vending of beverages in the foyer before concerts and during intermissions. Distinguishing the hall on a more purely musical note is its large pipe organ.

Acoustical impact was an overriding consideration in determining the specifications for the original seating. The architects examined the acoustical properties of different specifications for the wood and fabric before settling on the inaugural seating. Suntory Hall's management has subsequently revamped the upholstery every five years. Remodeling and expansion work in 2017 became an occasion for upgrading the lighting all throughout the auditorium.

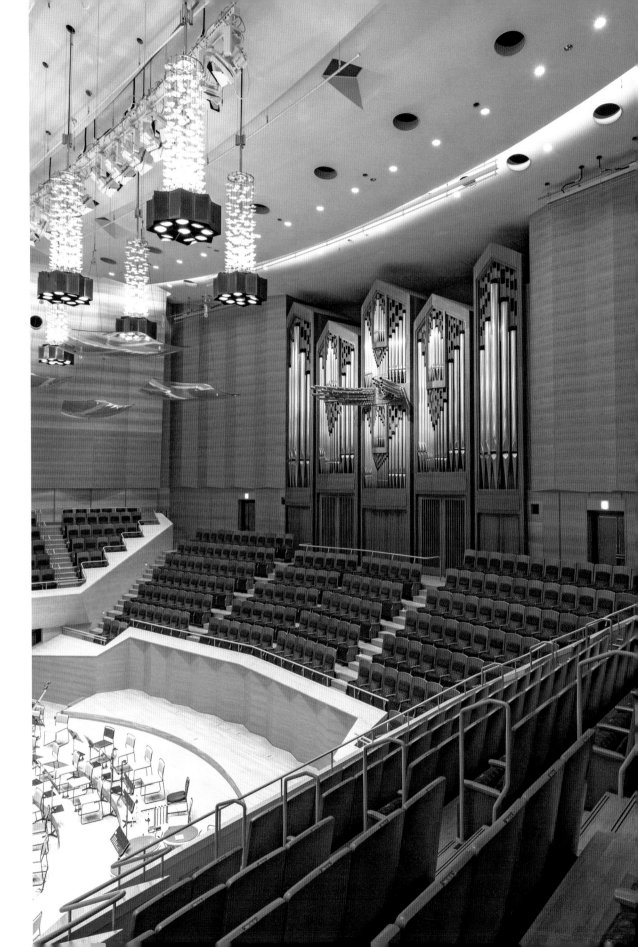

Orchard Hall

■ Location: Shibuya Ward, Tokyo ■ Owner: Tokyu Corporation ■ Architects: Ishimoto Architectural and Engineering Firm Inc.;
Tokyu Architects and Engineers Inc.; MIDI Sogo Sekkei Kenkyujo; Wilmotte Japan
■ Completed: 1989 ■ Remodeled: 2011 ■ Seating: 2,150

Bunkamura, home to Orchard Hall, was a Japanese pioneer in combining a concert hall with a movie theater, a playhouse, art galleries, and cafés. Orchard Hall was a Japanese first, meanwhile, as a "shoebox" design for a large concert hall. The reddish color theme for the hall evokes autumnal fertility, and the high ceiling and high walls nurture acoustics of fecund resonance. A stage-mounted, three-way "shelter" allows for accommodating different performance genres, such as classical music, opera, ballet, and popular music. The seats are high-backed, and the angle of the backs is sharper on the second level than on the first to optimize appreciation of performances.

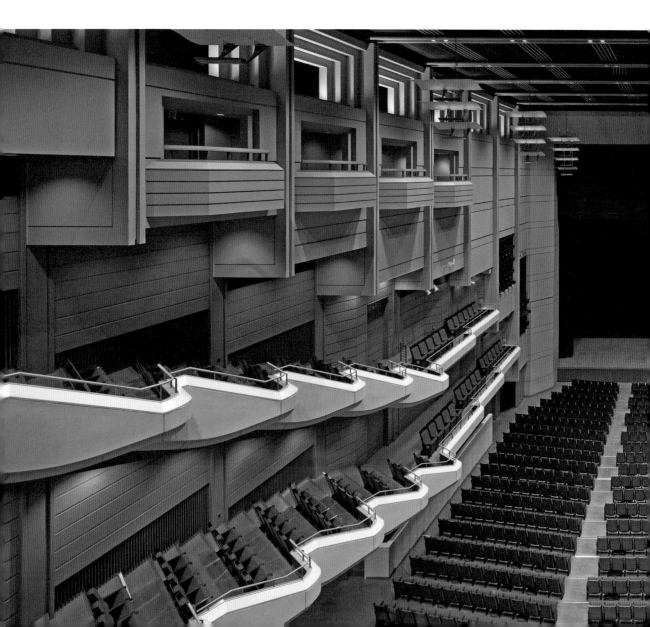

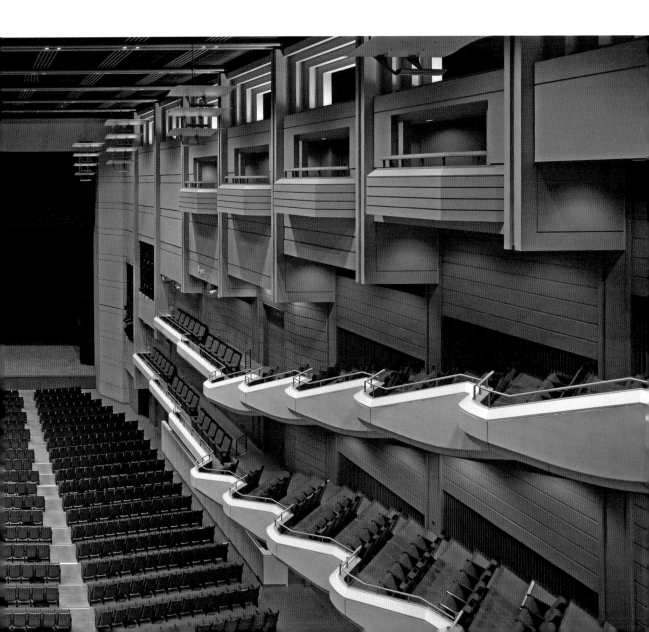

2

Exploring New Possibilities

Halls completed from 1990 to 1998

Saitama Arts Theater

■ Location: Saitama City, Saitama ■ Owner: Saitama Prefecture ■ Architect: Kohyama Atelier
■ Completed: 1994 ■ Remodeled: 2011
■ Seating: Main Theater, 776; Concert Hall, 604; Adaptable Theater, 346; Audio-Visual Hall, 150

The four performance halls at the Saitama Arts Theater are dedicated platforms for theatrical, musical, dance, and video productions. In the spirit of nurturing performance artists, the complex accompanies those halls with 12 rehearsal rooms, including one large enough to accommodate ensembles. The Saitama Arts Theater has earned an especially strong reputation for its offerings in contemporary dance and avant-garde theater. Its architect, Koyama Hisao, has underlined the complex's leading-edge orientation with lighting effects in the corridors and with an evocative rotunda.

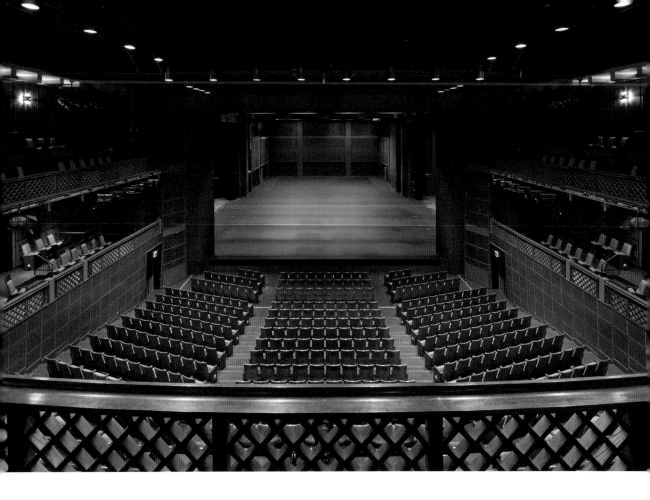

Aspiring in the Main Theater for Audience-Cast Solidarity and Audience Unity
Koyama Hisao Kohyama Atelier

This performance complex was born of an awareness that had taken hold in Japan by the 1990s. So-called multipurpose halls had sprung up in cities throughout the nation in the postwar era. Most of those halls were inadequate, however, for any single application and were more "purposeless" than "multipurpose." Reflection on that shortcoming kindled interest in creating specialized performance venues.

The Saitama Arts Theater was the first of the new wave. It was also the first theater project that I had undertaken. Tackling the project began with total immersion in the Eastern and Western traditions of theater architecture over the centuries. The project thus became an especially memorable undertaking for me personally.

Four specialized performance venues constitute the Saitama Arts Theater, of which the Main Theater (pp. 64–66) is for theatrical performances. That venue would have a broader, deeper, taller, and better-equipped stage than anything of its kind ever built in Japan. Another goal that we set for the theater was to facilitate an unprecedented bonding for audiences

with the performances. We aimed to nurture a sense of solidarity between the audience and the cast and a feeling of unity among the members of the audience.

Digitization had called into question the need for live theater. I was eager to demonstrate the irreplicable excitement of experiencing performance art in an architectural setting. Much in mind for me was the Japanese tradition of enjoying entertainments while partaking of food and spirits. I was determined to replicate something of that experience while contending with contemporary restraints. My design became an effort to engage the audience collectively and wholly in the performance.

The upshot of my stance was a layout that brought all of the seating within a 20-meter field of view. That included bringing the seating together in the most compact configuration and layout possible while retaining individual comfort.

My mandate in designing the Main Theater included accommodating a full range of productions, from classical to avant-garde, from traditional Japanese to Western and other cultural sources, from chamber

opera to full-blown ballet. We therefore strived in the interior decor to ensure harmony with any of the vast range of aesthetic possibilities. Likewise, we sought a universal admissibility in the colors and configurations of the furnishings.

Koyama equipped the Main Theater with a proscenium-style stage large enough for full-scale plays, musicals, operas, ballets, and dance productions. In the Adaptable Theater (top and middle, p. 67), he promoted audience engagement in performances with a bowl-like configuration for the seating. Audiences encounter a diversity of film and digital video work in the Audio-Visual Hall (bottom, p. 67) and of classical and other musical performances in the Concert Hall (bottom, p. 68).

The rotunda (p. 68), delineated by pillars and translucent glass blocks, is a circular courtyard in the center of the Saitama Arts Theater. Audiences traverse it to access the Main Theater, the Concert Hall, and the Adaptable Theater. The 5-meter-wide galleria (p. 69), illuminated by natural light that pours through its glass roof, stretches 100 meters through the complex. It passes by an information booth, office, rehearsal rooms, and the performers' entrances to the Concert Hall and Adaptable Theater. Its walls serve as exhibition space for artworks and as display space for performance posters.

Tokyo Metropolitan Theatre

■ Location: Toshima Ward, Tokyo ■ Owner: Tokyo Metropolitan Government
■ Architect: Ashihara Yoshinobu ■ Remodeling: MHS Planners, Architects and Engineers ■ Design assistance: Kohyama Atelier
■ Completed: 1990 ■ Remodeled: 2012 ■ Seating: Concert Hall, 1,999; Playhouse, 834; Theatre East, 286; Theatre West, 270

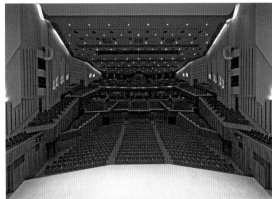

Ashihara Yoshinobu was an influential architect who famously described his artistic values in a Japanese bestseller published in English as *The Aesthetic Townscape*. He exercised those values convincingly in executing the commission for the Tokyo Metropolitan Theatre and an adjacent city park. Ashihara designed the building around a giant atrium, integrating the park into the design as an expansive plaza (p. 73).

The Concert Hall, which occupies the seventh, eighth, and ninth floors, features excellent acoustics and houses a large pipe organ. A one and a half year renovation completed in 2012 improved the acoustics by adding wooden ribs to the marble walls (pp. 70–71). The renovation also included broadening the stage, which has narrowed the gap between the performers and the audience.

In addition, the renovation included switching the chair seats to thicker cushions and replacing the plastic armrests with wooden ones. It included, too, adopting a different color tone for the upholstery in the seating on each floor. That has created a chromatic gradation that heightens the sense of depth.

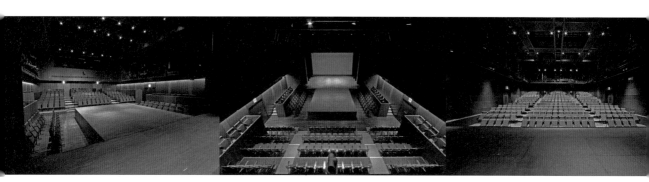

The proscenium-style Playhouse (top and middle, p. 72) is primarily for plays, musicals, and dance productions. It includes an orchestra pit that holds up to 60 musicians. Elegance is the theme, meanwhile, for the audience seating. The seat fabric takes on different colors when seen from different angles, lending an iridescent dynamism to the setting. In the multipurpose Theatre East and Theatre West (bottom, p. 72), movable stages and seating accommodates diverse modes of performance art.

Aichi Prefectural Art Theater

■ Location: Nagoya City, Aichi ■ Owner: Aichi Prefecture ■ Architect: A&T Associates
■ Completed: 1992 ■ Remodeled: 2019 ■ Seating: Main Theater, 2,480; Concert Hall, 1,800; Mini Theater, 330

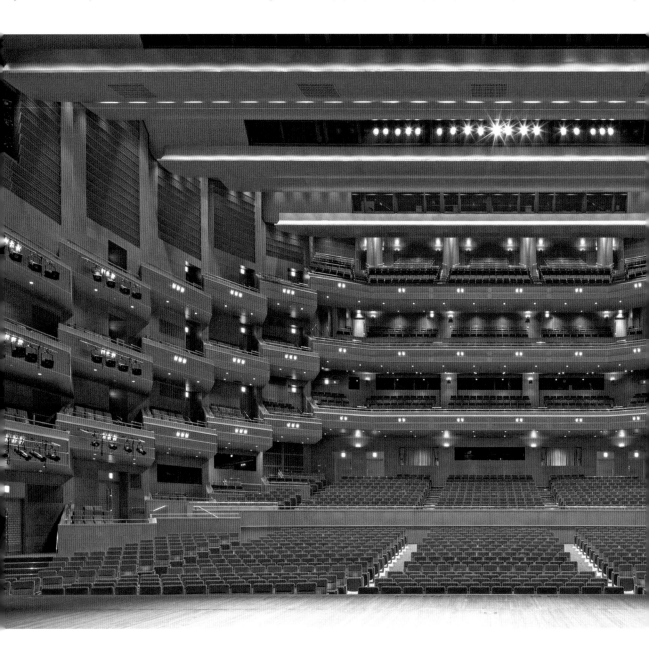

The Aichi Prefectural Art Theater is part of Nagoya's Aichi Arts Center, which also comprises the Aichi Prefectural Art Museum and the Aichi Prefectural Arts Promotion Service. In addition to its Main Theater (shown here), the Art Theater includes the 1,800-seat Concert Hall, the 330-seat (maximum capacity) Mini Theater, and rehearsal rooms. The Main Theater, which was Japan's first multistage theater and has a large lift in its main stage, can handle full-scale opera and ballet productions. Three levels of balcony seats surround the first- and second-floor seating in the horseshoe shape familiar in European opera houses. Remodeling work completed in April 2019 included shifting some of the front-section seats to a staggered seating arrangement and easing access by shortening the front row of seats on the second floor.

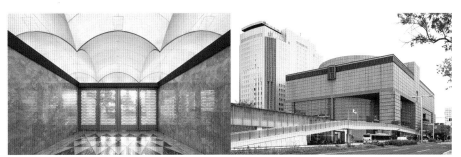

Hamarikyu Asahi Hall

■ Location: Chuo Ward, Tokyo ■ Owner: Asahi Shimbun Company ■ Architect: Takenaka Corporation
■ Completed: 1992 ■ Seating: 552

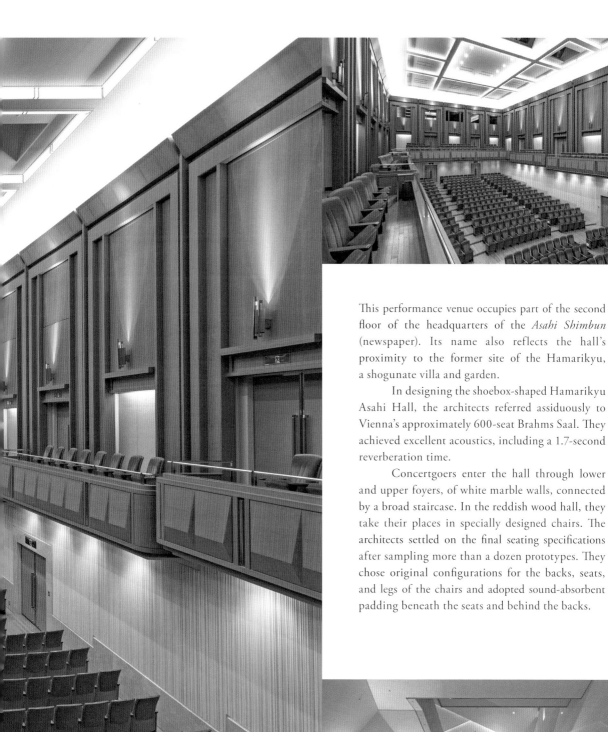

This performance venue occupies part of the second floor of the headquarters of the *Asahi Shimbun* (newspaper). Its name also reflects the hall's proximity to the former site of the Hamarikyu, a shogunate villa and garden.

In designing the shoebox-shaped Hamarikyu Asahi Hall, the architects referred assiduously to Vienna's approximately 600-seat Brahms Saal. They achieved excellent acoustics, including a 1.7-second reverberation time.

Concertgoers enter the hall through lower and upper foyers, of white marble walls, connected by a broad staircase. In the reddish wood hall, they take their places in specially designed chairs. The architects settled on the final seating specifications after sampling more than a dozen prototypes. They chose original configurations for the backs, seats, and legs of the chairs and adopted sound-absorbent padding beneath the seats and behind the backs.

Kamakura Performing Arts Center

■Location: Kamakura City, Kanagawa ■Owner: Kamakura City ■Architect: Ishimoto Architectural and Engineering Firm
■Completed: 1993 ■Remodeled: 2017 ■Seating: Main Hall, 1,500; Recital Hall, 600

Kamakura city officials conceived the Kamakura Performing Arts Center as a platform for enriching the cultural life of their city. The center comprises the 1,500-seat Main Hall, the 600-seat Recital Hall, three exhibition galleries, two rehearsal rooms, two meeting rooms, a banquet room, and a tatami-mat room.

Shadows cast by trees move across the building exterior in an eye-catching interplay with the striped walls (bottom, p. 81). Visitors can stroll across fine white gravel through bamboo in a courtyard redolent of Kamakura's heritage as Japan's former capital.

The shoebox-shaped Main Hall accommodates diverse performance events. It narrows slightly at each end to engender concert hall acoustics.

The Kamakura Performing Arts Center emerged in 2017 from a sweeping renovation. This included re-covering the upholstery on the Main Hall seating with iridescent fabric of blue, green, and coral-red threads on a yellow ground. It also included repainting the wooden portions of the seats in dark tones and installing vertical hand posts on the aisle seats on the steep, third level for safety (bottom left, p. 80).

Yokosuka Arts Theatre

- Location: Yokosuka City, Kanagawa ■ Owner: Yokosuka City ■ Architect: Kenzo Tange Associates
- Completed: 1994 ■ Seating: Yokosuka Art Theatre, 1,806; Yokosuka Bayside Pocket, 574

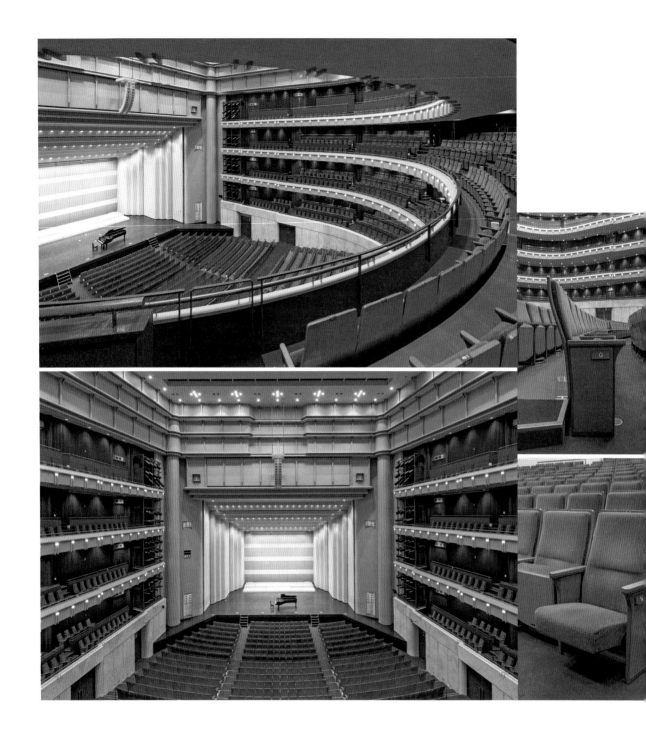

Yokosuka is where the US Navy's Commodore Matthew Perry disembarked in 1853 on his expedition to force the opening of Japan. It is the site today of a large US navy base, and signs of the US presence are highly visible throughout the city. The Yokosuka Arts Theatre stands on the former site of the US Navy's EM Club, which served enlisted men and spawned Japan's postwar rebirth of jazz. An annual summer jazz festival there pays homage to the site's musical history. The Yokosuka Art Theatre (pp. 82–84) is otherwise a venue for large-scale opera, ballet, and classical music performances.

Four-tiered balcony seating in a horseshoe-shaped concert hall was new to Japan when the Yokosuka Arts Theatre was completed in 1994 (the Aichi Prefectural Art Theater's Main Theater [pp. 74–75] having been a pioneering example), and the new facility garnered attention for its reference to European opera houses. Comfort was a primary consideration in choosing the seats, which are of standard specifications. The angle of the seating rows on the main levels is broad, and the positioning of the balcony seats is staggered to maximize the field of view.

A movable stage, movable seating, stackable chairs, and an upper tier of fixed seating provide the Yokosuka Arts Theatre's smaller hall, the Yokosuka Bayside Pocket [p. 85], with flexibility in accommodating different kinds of performances. The hall can become a proscenium-stage theater, an arena, or even a Kabuki-style theater. A 2017 renovation included refurbishing the upholstery with new sea-blue fabric and providing each chair with a number on the top of the back and on the front of the seat.

Tokyo International Forum

10

- Location: Chiyoda Ward, Tokyo ■ Owner: Tokyo Metropolis ■ Architect: Rafael Viñoly Architects
- Completed: 1996 ■ Remodeled: 2013 ■ Seating: 5,012 (Hall A)

The massive, glass-roofed Tokyo International Forum conference and exhibition complex comprises seven halls right in the middle of Tokyo's central business district. Designed by New York–based Rafael Viñoly Architects, the buildings combine bold exterior profiles with conscientiously devised interiors. Hall A is a 5,012-seat auditorium equipped with advanced audio and stage equipment that is as suitable for concerts as for conferences. It includes an interpreting booth and feeds to attendees' earphones in up to 16 languages. The chairs include writing stands and upholstery fabric of a high-grade, specially ordered weave.

Sinphonia Iwakuni

■ Location: Iwakuni City, Yamaguchi　■ Owner: Yamaguchi Prefecture　■ Architect: Otani Associates
■ Completed: 1996　■ Seating: Concert Hall, 1,205; Multipurpose Hall, 374

Sinphonia Iwakuni is part of a complex of prefectural government buildings and is an important node of cultural life in Yamaguchi. Its design is by the modernist architect Otani Sachio, who also designed the Kyoto International Conference Center. Sinphonia Iwakuni houses an art gallery, rehearsal rooms, and meeting rooms, as well as the Concert Hall and Multipurpose Hall. Incorporating a vibration-absorbing structure for the roof and outer walls has shielded the facility from the noise and vibration that emanate from a nearby passenger train line and US Air Force base.

The Concert Hall (pp. 90–91) is a paragon for western Japan of state-of-the-art stage equipment and lucid acoustics. It is a venue for high-profile, international presentations and conferences, as well as concerts. The Multipurpose Hall (p. 92) accommodates diverse events flexibly with a movable stage and with seating that can retract into the floor.

Ryutopia (Niigata City Performing Arts Center)

■ Location: Niigata City, Niigata ■ Owner: Niigata City ■ Architect: Itsuko Hasegawa Atelier
■ Completed: 1998 ■ Seating: Concert Hall, 1,884; Theater, 903; Noh Theater, 387

"An island in a forest" is the image that inspired the architect Hasegawa Itsuko in designing Ryutopia. In keeping with that inspiration, Hasegawa supported a glass shell with tree-like pillars and placed a verdant garden atop the building. The result is a landscape that blends organically with the adjacent Hakusan Park and the nearby Shinanogawa river.

In the arena-style Concert Hall, the audience seating completely surrounds the stage. The curvature of the walls and ceiling yield excellent acoustics, which have lured the Tokyo Symphony Orchestra for an annual series of six concerts. Further enhancing the acoustics are sound-absorbing louvers installed beneath the seats. Those louvers, refined through repeated testing under the guidance of Yamaha Corporation, help ensure acoustical consistency between rehearsals and concerts. Beautifying the seating is upholstery fabric of complex Jacquard weave.

Nara Centennial Hall

■ Location: Nara City, Nara ■ Owner: Nara City ■ Architect: Arata Isozaki & Associates
■ Completed: 1998 ■ Seating: Main Hall, 2,381; Harmony Hall, 434

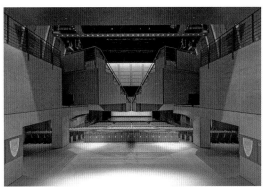

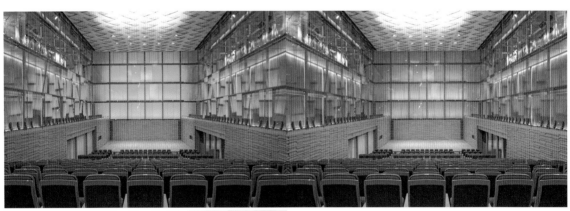

Nara City built the multipurpose Centennial Hall to mark the 100th anniversary of its incorporation as a municipality. The architect Isozaki Arata envisioned the hall, which stands before Nara's central train station, as a "culture boat." Handling the architectural engineering was Kawaguchi Mamoru. He proposed the pantadome structure of 240 precast concrete panels employed for the curved exterior, which Isozaki textured with brick surfacing.

The Main Hall (pp. 98–101) accommodates concerts and conferences. Enhancing its flexibility is rail mounting for the seating blocks. The smaller, 434-seat Harmony Hall (p. 102) is a glass-walled venue that features superior acoustics. Different-colored lighting is available to generate event-specific atmosphere. Whereas the seats in the Main Hall are simple chairs with exposed back panels (p.100), those in the Harmony Hall have upholstered, sound-absorbent backs.

Kitara (Sapporo Concert Hall)

■ Location: Sapporo City, Hokkaido ■ Owner: Sapporo City ■ Architect: Docon Co., Ltd.
■ Completed: 1997 ■ Seating: Main Hall, 2,008; Chamber Music Hall, 453

Sapporo's Nakajima Park, known for its iris pond and historic buildings, furnishes the backdrop for the Kitara performance venue. Kitara's Main Hall is the home ground for the Sapporo Symphony Orchestra and hosts performances by a global cast of large ensembles. The name *Kitara* is a play on the Greek *kithara* (lute) and the Japanese *kita* (north), the latter being a reference to Hokkaido's latitude.

A three-part work in white marble by the Hokkaido-born sculptor Yasuda Kan holds court at the Kitara entrance, at the entrance to the Main Hall, and in the Main Hall foyer. Concert attendees enter the Main Hall via an opera staircase through an atrium (bottom, right, p. 107). A vineyard-style layout establishes common ground for the audience and performers.

Wood native to Hokkaido is an embracing assurance in the Main Hall. Dominating the view in that hall is a pipe organ crafted over two years by France's Daniel Kern Manufacture d'Orgues and designed to evoke Hokkaido conifers (top, p. 107). The armrests and backs of the Main Hall's seats, meanwhile, are of a variety of Hokkaido birch that has become difficult to obtain. Three-rowed cushioning lends a distinctive look to the seat backs.

Yokohama Minato Mirai Hall

- Location: Yokohama City, Kanagawa ■ Owner: Yokohama City ■ Architect: Nikken Sekkei Ltd.
- Completed: 1998 ■ Seating: Main Hall, 2,020; Small Hall, 440

Yokohama has accomplished a spectacular harborside renewal with Minato Mirai, a vast redevelopment project. A tremendously popular tourist destination, Minato Mirai is also a cultural magnet, thanks to such attractions as the Yokohama Minato Mirai Hall and the Yokohama Museum of Art. The Main Hall at the

Minato Mirai Hall combines a shoebox shape with arena-style seating. Its three-level seating positions all of the 2,000-plus seats within 33.5 meters of the stage, engendering a compelling immediacy. Ornamenting the mahogany case of the 4,623-pipe organ, nicknamed Lucy, are carved reliefs of seagulls.

The seats in the Main Hall have built-in air-conditioning (bottom, right, p. 110), which was a seating breakthrough of its day. Mounted under the natural incline of the seat backs, the slim air-conditioning units are spatially unimposing. Localizing temperature management is quieter and consumes less energy than central air-conditioning.

Biwako Hall Center for the Performing Arts, Shiga

■ Location: Otsu City, Shiga ■ Owner: Shiga Prefecture ■ Architect: AXS Satow Inc.
■ Completed: 1998 ■ Seating: Main Theatre, 1,848; Theatre, 804; Ensemble Hall, 323

Offerings at the Biwako Hall Center for the Performing Arts, Shiga, extend beyond performances. Visitors can also stroll through the adjacent city park to the namesake lake (Japan's largest) and relax in the rooftop garden. Even in the foyer, visitors enjoy vistas of the lake.

Audiences in the Main Theatre (pp. 112–115) witness performances on a stage fully configured with left and right side stages and a back stage, in addition to the center stage. The full configuration allows for productions to tap a vast spectrum of expressive possibilities. Acoustical considerations figured influentially in the specifications for the seating, which is of hefty-gauge, special-order construction. Ornamenting the fabric covering of the upholstery is a woven rendering of the rhododendron, Shiga's prefectural flower.

The interior of the smaller, 804-seat Theatre (top, p. 116) is a balanced harmony of dark colors. In the Ensemble Hall (bottom, p. 116), the seating's emerald-green upholstery strikes a tonal contrast with the wooden side paneling.

3

Giving Audiences Their Due
Halls completed from 1999 to 2010

Ala (Kani Public Arts Center)

■ Location: Kani City, Gifu   ■ Owner: Kani City   ■ Architect: Kohyama Atelier
■ Completed: 2002   ■ Seating: Sora no Hall, 1,019; Small Theater, 311

Kani City officials engaged the citizenry in the development of the Kani Public Arts Center, Ala, through workshops at three stages: conceptualizing the facility, developing the design, and commencing operation of the completed center. The architect Koyama Hisao accommodated the requests of the citizenry under a broad roof. Complementing the multipurpose Sora no Hall and a smaller performance theater are a video theater; a reception room; three music rehearsal rooms; a drama rehearsal room; an exhibition gallery; a children's room; two workshop rooms (one floored with Japanese-style tatami mats, the other furnished with tables and chairs); a classroom; a printing room; a video editing room; three lofts (art, drama, and music); a woodworking room; and a restaurant.

Koyama achieved an intimacy in the Sora no Hall (sora refers to "space," as in the cosmos) by positioning all of the seats within about 23 meters of the stage. He incorporated the hall seating into the architecture by leaving exposed structural parts and screws. Red, suede-like upholstery and air-conditioning vents in the seat backs impart a touch of luxury and advanced functionality.

Inclusive Theater Management for Enriching the Community: *Accompanying Population Growth with Social Bonding*

Ei Kisei Director, Ala (Kani Public Arts Center)
        Artistic supervisor, Ala theaters

Kani City's population increased by 937 over the year to March 2019, to 102,229. That increase belies the depopulation that plagues regional municipalities throughout Japan. The growth figures thus took me by surprise, though I had taken note of convincing signs of vitality in the city in recent years. New homes were springing up on newly developed tracts of residential land, and the cheerful voices of children going to and from school evoked a pulsing vitality.

What had prompted me to check the population figures for Kani was a December 2018 conversation with the mayor. He had expressed a desire to position the Kani Public Arts Center, Ala, as a driving force in fostering community spirit.

Kani had suffered a population decline after the global financial crisis of 2008. Automobile manufacturing and other industries employed thousands of ethnic Japanese Brazilians in Gifu, who enjoyed favored access to working visas, and some 2,000 Brazilians left Kani on account of job losses caused by the financial crisis. As a result, the population fell well below 99,000, but it had recovered to more than 102,000, as I have noted, 10 years later.

Several factors have figured in Kani's population growth. Young couples who have small children are moving to the city from villages in the hill country nearby. Kani has also had an influx of Filipino families. And some of Gifu's Brazilian residents who have obtained permanent-residence visas are building homes here. Reinforcing Kani's appeal are free medical care for children up to junior high school, regardless of family income, and, in contrast with Japan's large cities, no waiting-line access to day care centers for preschool children.

Ala is doing its part, nurturing community spirit in line with the mayor's expectations. It hosts world-class theatrical productions and more than 460 community-inclusion programs a year. Through our Ala Community Vitality Project, we hold diverse activities to forestall the alienation that can result from widening income disparity. Our focus is on transcending economic, social, and psychological barriers to engage with everyone in the community. Ala is not a temple for art but, rather, a home for people. We are striving to help position Kani as an inviting and fulfilling place to live.

Chino Cultural Complex

■ Location: Chino City, Nagano ■ Owner: Chino City ■ Architect: Furuya Nobuaki (NASCA)
■ Completed: 2005 ■ Seating: Multi Hall, 780; Concert Hall, 300

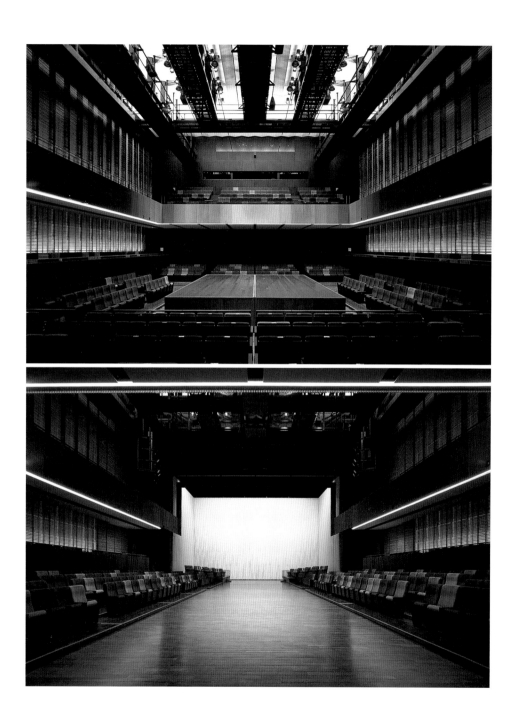

In store at the Chino Cultural Complex are theatrical and musical performances in the Multi Hall and Concert Hall, exhibitions of work by local artists in the museum, and published works in the library. The architect Furuya Nobuaki designed the glass-walled complex, which runs parallel to a local train station, as a community-engagement facility. Here, the ordinary activity of commuting overlaps the wondrous stimuli of art. Movable seating in the Multi Hall (pp. 126–130) allows for varying the layout to accommodate diverse genres of performance art.

All of the seats in the Chino Cultural Complex's Multi Hall are of original design, including the fabric of soft-napped weave. Interspersing occasional seats of pale purple in the field of mainly dark-gray seating lends a visual syncopation to the setting. The balcony seats (top, p. 130) allow the occupants to pivot freely in accordance with the layout and the flow of the action below.

Ishikawa Ongakudo

■ Location: Kanazawa City, Ishikawa ■ Owner: Ishikawa Prefecture ■ Architect: Ashihara Architect and Associates
■ Completed: 2001 ■ Seating: Concert Hall, 1,560; Hogaku Hall, 727; Koryu Hall, 300

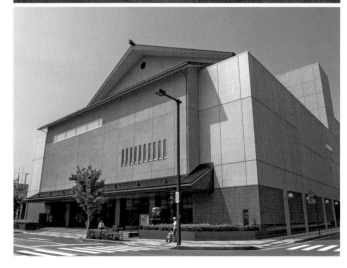

Kanazawa's central train station is a daring composite of temple-style wooden architecture and modernistic glass. Standing beside the station's east plaza, the Ishikawa Ongakudo houses three halls of contrasting orientation. The Hogaku (Japanese music) Hall welcomes visitors with a traditionally styled façade, and the Concert Hall presents a glass-faced entrance (top, p. 135). Access to the Koryu (interchange) Hall is through an underground passageway between the Ishikawa Ongakudo and the station.

The Hogaku Hall (pp. 132–133) features a rotating stage equipped with 12 lifts. Its curtain, emblazoned with a pine tree and azalea motif, is of Kaga *yuzen*, a variety of resist-dyed silk native to Kanazawa. The seating features cherry blossom–patterned upholstery and lacquered wood from the nearby city of Wajima, famed for its lacquerware. Each seat is deeper than usual to accommodate the *obi* sashes of kimono-clad female audience members.

Classical music is the focus of the Concert Hall (pp. 134–135), which hosts an international mix of performances and is home to Orchestra Ensemble Kanazawa. Ornamenting the case of the pipe organ is *maki-e* (sprinkled picture) lacquer work by Wajima artists. Lacquer from the region coats the wood-grain walls, improving the acoustics and fostering a sense of warmth. Enlivening the seating upholstery are red and orange images of Kanazawa's turning leaves.

Wel Tobata

■ Location: Kitakyushu City, Fukuoka ■ Owner: Kitakyushu City ■ Architect: Azusa Sekkei Co., Ltd.
■ Completed: 2002 ■ Seating: Main Hall, 800; Hitachi Metals Memorial Hall, 300

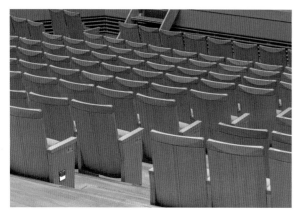

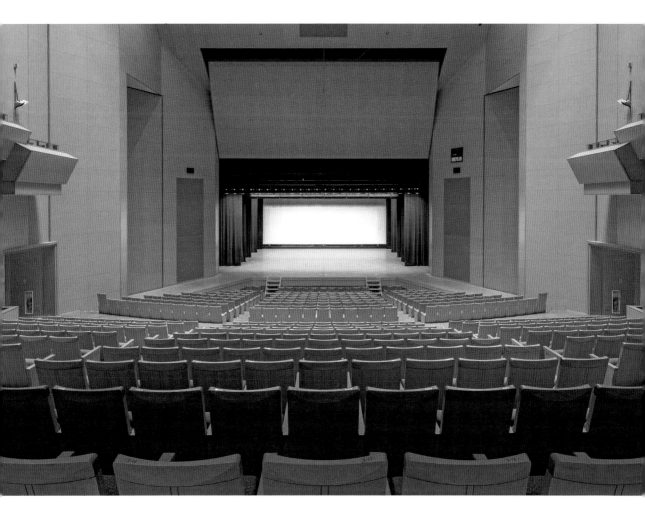

Wel Tobata comprises a building that houses two performance halls and a building that houses some 40 public-welfare organizations. Walkways connect both buildings conveniently to Tobata's central station and to a nearby retail complex.

The Main Hall (pp. 136–137) has a rotating stage fitted with large and small lifts and with movable acoustic panels. It accommodates concerts, large-scale theatrical productions, and other kinds of performances. Distinguishing the chairs (p. 137) are three-centimeter-thick sideboards of white birch.

In the Hitachi Metals Memorial Hall (pp. 138–139), the forward rows of seating trace arcs, and the individual seats display rounded contours. Echoing the contoured geometry are the curved relief in the seat backs and aisle-facing sideboards.

National Theatre Okinawa

■Location: Urasoe City, Okinawa　■Owner: Japan Arts Council　■Architect: Shin Takamatsu Architect and Associates Co., Ltd.
■Completed: 2003　■Seating: Large Theatre, 632; Small Theatre, 255

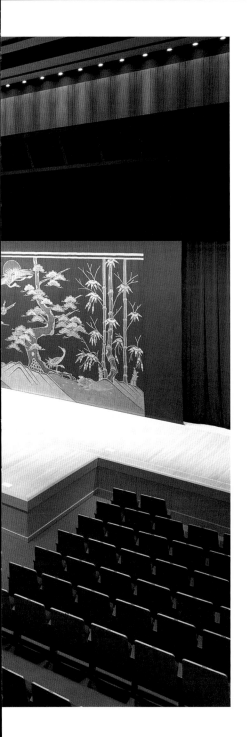

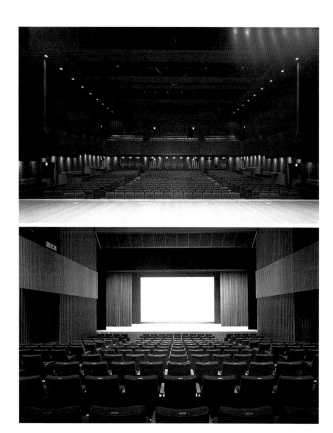

Opened in 2004, the National Theatre Okinawa became Japan's sixth national theater. Its founding purpose was to propagate Okinawa's Kumiodori tradition of theatrical art and other Okinawa traditions of performance art. Kumiodori arose in Okinawa's Ryukyu Kingdom (15th century–1879) as an expression of welcome for official delegations from China. It has received a designation from the Japanese government as an important intangible cultural property.

The National Theatre Okinawa honors Okinawan culture with its architecture, as well as with its performance offerings. It features allusions in concrete to the deep, *amahaji* eaves and the *chinibu* woven-bamboo windows that exemplify the semitropical nature of Okinawan architecture.

In the Large Theatre (p. 140), the movable stage can project into the audience seating and can also sport a *hanamichi* walkway that extends through the audience seating between the stage and the back of the theater. That allows for deploying authentic layouts for Kumiodori and Kabuki performances. The Small Theatre (top, p. 141) provides an intimate environment for recitals and performances by small ensembles.

Kitakyushu Performing Arts Center

■ Location: Kitakyushu City, Fukuoka ■ Owner: Kitakyushu City ■ Architect: Nihon Sekkei
■ Completed: 2003 ■ Seating: Main Hall, 1,269; Theater, 700; Small Theater, 216

Kitakyushu City, long known as a center of heavy industry, is working to cultivate an identity as a cultural center. Its efforts have included developing the Riverwalk Kitakyushu retail and cultural complex in the city's Kokurakita Ward. That complex includes movie theaters; the Kitakyushu Municipal Museum of Art; the Riverwalk Gallery; and, atop the complex on the fifth and sixth floors, the Kitakyushu Performing Arts Center.

The Main Hall in the Kitakyushu Performing Arts Center (pp. 142–143) is of proscenium-stage design and hosts musicals, ballets, classical music, and popular music. Its seating evokes an ingratiating atmosphere. Dotted vortices enliven the dark green upholstery fabric, and the reddish wood fittings are of pleasingly curved contours. The air-conditioning vents merge unassertively with the seat backs.

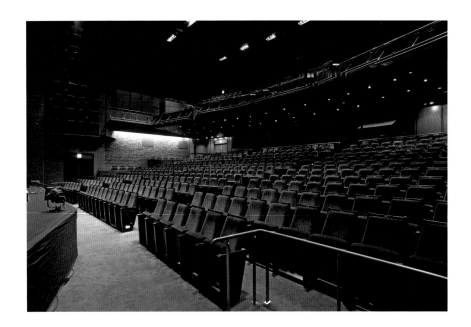

Kitakyushu boasts a rich tradition of theatrical arts, and that tradition lives on in the Kitakyushu Performing Arts Center's Theater (top, p. 144). The Theater seating, which includes balcony seats, is chic. A lattice pattern embellishes the dark blue upholstery fabric, and the chair fittings are metallic. As in the Main Hall, the seats have built-in air-conditioning. In the Small Theater (p. 145), the stage and seating are movable, allowing for layout flexibility. The interior is of neutral tones in keeping with the eclectic mix of performances. Fortifying the tone of the upholstery fabric are three shades of brown and gray thread.

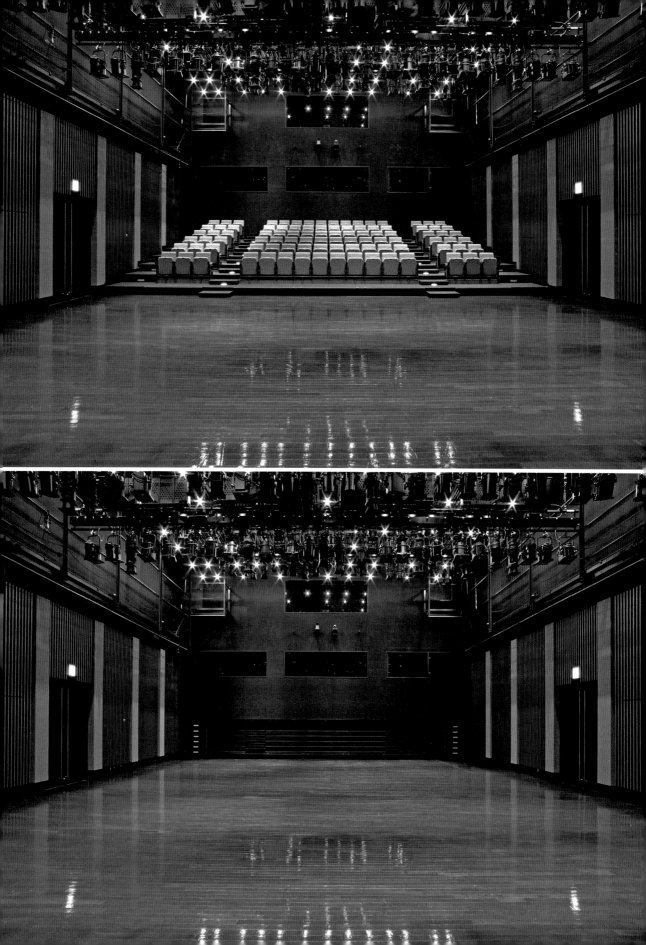

Muza (Kawasaki Symphony Hall)

■ Location: Kawasaki City, Kanagawa ■ Owner: Kawasaki City
■ Completed: 2003 ■ Remodeled: 2013 ■ Seating: 1,997

Kawasaki Symphony Hall, Muza, has won acclaim for its acoustics from a host of musical luminaries, including Sir Simon Rattle, the music director of the London Symphony Orchestra. It occupies the 4th to 7th floors of the 27-story Muza Kawasaki Central Tower. That building connects via an elevated walkway to Kawasaki's central train station and has become a Kawasaki landmark as a locus of advanced technology, information, and culture. A vineyard-style design wraps the Muza seating on the first level completely around the stage in an upward-spiraling pattern. The steep incline on the top level has entailed adjusting the dimensions of the seating on a seat-by-seat basis. Varying the color of the upholstery fabric from bright red on the first level through darker reds on the second and third levels to black on the fourth level has emphasized the sweep of the hall. Improvements made in the seating in 2013 and the addition of vertical handles to the aisle seats in 2017 have eased access.

Matsumoto Performing Arts Centre

■ Location: Matsumoto City, Nagano ■ Owner: Matsumoto City ■ Architect: Toyo Ito & Associates, Architects
■ Completed: 2004 ■ Seating: Grand Hall, 1,800; Special Theatre, 360; Small Hall, 288

Light emanates from the Matsumoto Performing Arts Centre though an irregular pattern of glass inlay in the outer walls (top, p. 153). Entry is by way of a meandering course in the manner of a woodland path. The stage in the Grand Hall (pp. 150–152), equipped with stages on both sides, is broad enough for opera productions. A gradation from bright red to black that unfolds across the seating and on the walls focuses attention on the stage. The seating design echoes the curvature of the four levels of balconies.

Behind the stage in the Grand Hall is the Special Theatre (middle, p. 153), complete with rollback seating. The Small Hall (bottom, left, p. 153) brings the audience and performers together in a boxed, common space. Theatre Park, the second-floor lobby, offers respite before and after performances and during intermissions. On clear days, the observation deck rewards visitors with spectacular views of Nagano's alpine scenery.

Kibou Hall (Sakata Civic Hall)

■Location: Sakata City, Yamagata ■Owner: Sakata City ■Architect. Toshio Homma and Associates
■Completed: 2004 ■Seating: Great Hall, 1,287; Small Hall, 150

Sakata, a harbor city in northern Honshu, opened in 1962 one of Japan's first civic halls of 1,000-seat capacity. Forty-two years later, it replaced the aging structure with Kibou Hall on a site adjacent to the old civic hall. Kibou Hall stands in a scenic district near Sakata's historic Sankyo Soko rice storehouses. Its architect, the Yamagata native Homma Toshio, earned acclaim with works that harmonize with their setting, including the Yamagata Museum of Art and the Tohoku University of Art and Design.

The Great Hall is a multipurpose venue. Serving Yamagata's robust demand for classical music was a design priority, however, and the hall boasts superior acoustics. Innovative devices employed in the interior design contribute to the acoustical performance. Wall panels evoke beautifully the sails on the single-mast *kitamaefune* cargo vessels that served Sakata Port from the 17th to 19th centuries and optimize the hall's sound diffusion and resonance. Similarly, the undulating ceiling furnishes a sound-optimizing function while evoking aesthetically the violent churning of the Japan Sea. Also serving to enhance the acoustics is the extensive wood surfacing.

Built into each seat back in the Great Hall is an air-conditioning unit. The Small Hall, meanwhile, has a movable stage to accommodate a diversity of performance formats.

Sunport Hall Takamatsu

■ Location: Takamatsu City, Kagawa   ■ Owner: Takamatsu City
■ Architects: MHS Planners, Architects and Engineers; NTT Facilities Inc.; A & T Associates; Design Division, Taisei Corporation
■ Completed: 2004   ■ Seating: Main Hall, 1,312; No. 1 Small Hall, 312; No. 2 Small Hall, 500

The three performance halls of Sunport Hall Takamatsu occupy the floors of the 7-story Hall Building in the Sunport Takamatsu Symbol Tower. That building connects to the adjacent, 30-story Tower Building via a promenade through a semi-enclosed atrium.

Audiences partake of a variety of musical and theatrical performances in the Main Hall (pp. 156–157). That hall is of a proscenium configuration and has flexible seating adaptable to layouts of 1,312, 1,222, or 1,034 seats. Takamatsu faces the Seto Naikai inland sea at the north end of the island of Shikoku, and the Main Hall curtain is a brilliant mix of gold and bronze tones that symbolize the radiance of the Seto Naikai water and the pristine clarity of the seaside air. Audiences luxuriate in the comfortable seats, which include built-in air-conditioning.

The No. 1 Small Hall is likewise of proscenium design and is primarily for theatrical performances. Its counterpart, the No. 2 Small Hall, is a flexible venue that accommodates a vast array of performance genres. Sunport Hall Takamatsu also contains 12 conference rooms, three rehearsal halls, six practice rooms, and a rooftop wood deck for taking in views of the Seto Naikai and the city.

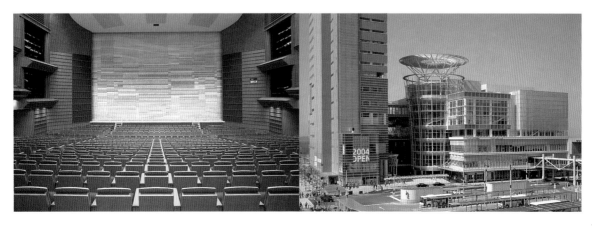

Hyogo Performing Arts Center

■ Location: Nishinomiya City, Hyogo ■ Owner: Hyogo Prefecture ■ Architect: Nikken Sekkei
■ Completed: 2005 ■ Seating: Grand Hall, 2,141; Theater, 800; Recital Hall, 417

Nishinomiya City was much a part of the swath of Hyogo devastated in the Great Hanshin Earthquake of 1995. The Hyogo Performing Arts Center opened there 10 years after the disaster as a symbol of spiritual and cultural rebirth. Its rhythmically spaced columns and its glass ceiling bespeak an architectural minimalism, and an environmental sensitivity is on view in the power generation with photovoltaic units, the rooftop greenery, and the recirculation of rainwater. The Grand Hall (pp. 158–159) is a venue for orchestral concerts and for ballet and opera productions and other large-scale performances. Its natural wood interior and the black fabric seating upholstery integrate the four-level hall in an organic whole.

Theatrical productions, musicals, and traditional Japanese performance arts are the main emphasis in the Hyogo Performing Arts Center's Theater (p. 160). The Theater accommodates individually assembled stages, and its acoustics deliver performers' lines faithfully to the ears of every member of the audience.

In the Recital Hall (p. 161), audiences enjoy chamber music, jazz, and other musical genres on a modest scale. The gently curved walls and ceiling of the arena-style hall favor good acoustics.

In all three halls, the seating features the same basic configuration and the same herringbone upholstery fabric. A difference of note is that between the black upholstery fabric and dark mahogany wood in the Grand Hall and Recital Hall and the red upholstery fabric and fir wood in the Theater.

MJ Hall (Miyakonojo General Cultural Hall)

■Location: Miyakonojo City, Miyazaki ■Owner: Miyakonojo City ■Architect: NTT Facilities
■Completed: 2006 ■Seating: Large Hall, 1,461; Small Hall, 682

Standing near the municipal park Kambashira Koen just minutes on foot from the city of Miyakonojo's central station is Miyakonojo General Cultural, or MJ, Hall. It comprises two concert and theatrical halls, three rehearsal rooms, two recording rooms, and several other rooms for meetings and other purposes. The range of facilities reflects citizen input at each stage of the planning and designing of MJ Hall.

Plays are the chief fare in the darkish wood-grain interior of the Small Hall (pp. 162–163). The Y in the upholstery of each seat back symbolizes an arrow and is a reference to the Miyakonojo tradition of crafting archery bows.

Opera and orchestral performances are the mainstay in the light-colored wood-grain interior of the Large Hall (pp. 164–165), which includes an orchestra pit and a fully configured stage. The Large Hall also accommodates theatrical performances and lectures. Its seating upholstery exhibits the same arrow symbol seen in the Small Hall seating, and air-conditioning vents in each seat back furnish localized comfort management.

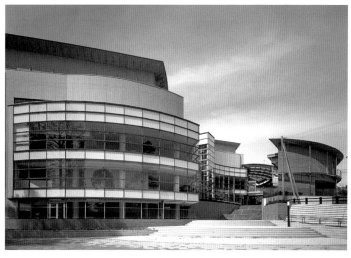

Popolo (Mihara Performing Arts Center)

■ Location: Mihara City, Hiroshima   ■ Owner: Mihara City   ■ Architect: Maki and Associates
■ Completed: 2007   ■ Seating: 1,209

Greeting visitors to the Mihara Performing Arts Center, Popolo, is a glass pavilion that stretches beneath a stainless steel dome. Popolo borders Miyaura Park, in central Mihara, on two sides. A café that overlooks a courtyard beside the foyer is open to everyone, regardless of whether they are attending a Popolo event. In keeping with the spirit of community engagement, the rehearsal hall and practice rooms are also available for members of the general public to use. Popolo accommodates a comprehensive range of musical and theatrical productions with a fully configured stage, including a fly tower, acoustical panels, and an orchestra pit. The polygonal ceiling functions acoustically to enhance the resonance in the hall and visually to unite the audience and performers.

As for the seating, the trapezoidal seat backs broaden downward, and the V-shaped openings under the armrests echo the polygonal theme of the hall interior. Each seat rests on a single, central pillar, which maximizes the space underneath.

Rias Hall (Ofunato Civic Cultural Center and Library)

■ Location: Ofunato City, Iwate ■ Owner: Ofunato City ■ Architect: Chiaki Arai Urban and Architecture Design
■ Completed: 2008 ■ Seating: Large Hall, 1,100; Multi Space, 244

168

Ofunato, known for its ria coast, lies at the southern end of the Sanriku Fukko (Reconstruction) National Park on the northeast edge of Honshu. And references to the ria coast and to the sea beyond recur throughout the architecture of Rias Hall (Ofunato Civic Cultural Center and Library). Those references manifest in numerous semiprivate spaces, which reinforce the sense of accessibility.

The Rias Hall complex includes the Large Hall and Multi Space for live events and movie screenings, a restaurant, and the library. Its architect, Arai Chiaki, convened a series of community workshops to elicit citizens' ideas for the complex, and he incorporated a lot of those ideas in the design. That has nurtured a strong sense of grass roots engagement with the end product.

Shibuya Cultural Center Owada

■Location: Shibuya Ward, Tokyo ■Owner: Shibuya Ward ■Architect: NTT Facilities Inc.
■Completed: 2010 ■Seating: Sakura Hall, 735; Densho Hall, 345

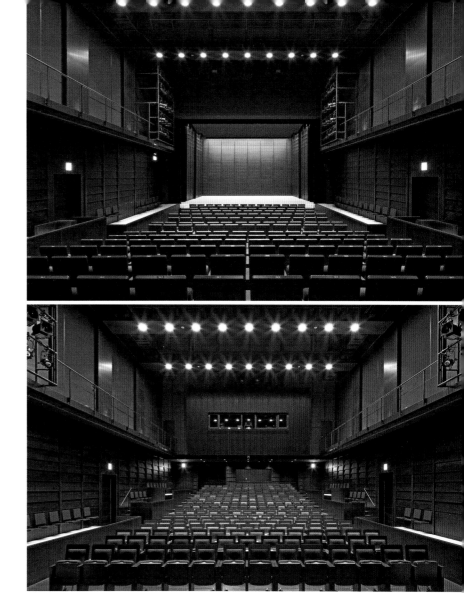

Two musical and theatrical halls, a library, a nursery school, a gender equality and diversity center, and a planetarium occupy Shibuya Cultural Center Owada. Visitors enter the 12-story center, which stands on the former site of Owada Elementary School, through a wide-open atrium on the first floor. And architects have designed the building to support unrestrained movement among the tenant facilities. Musical concerts are the main fare in Sakura Hall (pp. 172–174), where the shoebox configuration favors good acoustics. Woven into the upholstery fabric of the seating are the hall's namesake sakura (cherry) blossoms. Densho Hall (p. 175) is a flexible venue that can accommodate theater, dance, cinema, and lectures. On hand for traditional Japanese performance genres are a *hanamichi* walkway and box seats. Supplementary seating ordinarily stored in the walls is available as necessary.

Shinkabukiza

■Location: Osaka City, Osaka ■Owner: Shinkabukiza Co., Ltd. ■Architect: Nihon Sekkei
■Completed: 2010 ■Seating: 1,453

Shinkabukiza moved in 2006 from its Osaka home of long standing in a then-aging theater to the newly built Uehommachi Yufura building (bottom, left, p. 179) in the city's Uehommachi district. Its new theater occupies the sixth to eighth floors of the 13-story building.

The Shinkabukiza theater, accessible directly from the Osaka-Uehommachi passenger rail station, complements its Kabuki offerings with period-drama plays, omnibus productions of Japanese popular music, and solo concerts by famous musical entertainers. It has a traditional Kabuki layout, with a rotating stage and a *hanamichi* walkway that reaches from the stage to the back of the theater.

Light pours into the foyer through floor-to-ceiling windows latticed in a cusped gable pattern. Inside, three levels of seating position all the members of the audience close to the stage in broad, shallow tiers. Emblazoning the curtain colorfully are the birds and flora of a painting by the noted *nihonga* artist Uemura Atsushi (top, p. 178).

Shimane Arts Center

■ Location: Masuda City, Shimane ■ Owner: Shimane Prefecture ■ Architect: Naito Architect and Associates
■ Completed: 2005 ■ Seating: Large Hall, 1,500; Small Hall, 400

Excellent acoustics and a big stage equipped to handle opera and ballet productions distinguish the Large Hall (pp. 182–183) at Shimane Prefecture's Iwami Arts Theater. That theater complex shares the Shimane Arts Center with the Iwami Arts Museum.

Naito Hiroshi, the center's designer, designed the complex as "architecture that would converse with the city." He positioned the Iwami Arts Theater's Large and Small Halls, the Iwami Art Museum, and a restaurant around a courtyard and covered their roofs and walls with *Sekishu-gawara*, a lustrous, rust-colored tile produced in the Iwami district since around 1600. Ordinarily, a shallow reflecting pool fills the center of the courtyard, but removing the water makes the entire courtyard available for outdoor events.

The Small Hall of the Iwami Arts Theater (p. 184) is for small-scale plays, chamber music, and traditional Japanese performance arts. Here and in the Large Hall, the seating features built-in air-conditioning and textured upholstery fabric evocative of *Sekishu-gawara* tile.

4

Blurring the Line between Performers and Audience

Halls completed since 2011

Tetto (Kamaishi Civic Hall)

■ Location: Kamaishi City, Iwate ■ Owner: Kamaishi City ■ Architect: aat + yukomizu architects, inc.
■ Completed: 2017 ■ Seating: Hall A, 838; Hall B, About 200

Today's Kamaishi Civic Hall, Tetto, is the successor to a facility destroyed in the Great East Japan Earthquake of 2011. It incorporates several features for encouraging interchange, such as a glass-roofed plaza at the entrance (p. 190) and stroll ways through the building. The wood surfaces of the walls and ceiling in Hall A undulate in wavy forms that animate the setting. Stowing the 480 first-level seats allows for linking Halls A and B in a single large arena (bottom, p. 190). On additionally stowing the 358 upper-level seats, the two halls can merge with the lobby and the plaza in an arena 77 meters deep (p. 191).

A Role for Theater Seating in Reconstruction in the Wake of Disaster

Yokomizo Makoto Architect

An opportunity arose in the late 1990s for me to think anew about performance hall seating. I was working at Toyo Ito & Associates, Architects, and participated in designing the Sendai Mediatheque, a public-sector hub of artistic activity completed in 2000. The building would include a 180-seat theater for screening films, and I was responsible for the seating.

I marveled at how national character manifested in seating products, just as in automobiles. Products from the venerable French manufacturer of seating Quinette Gallay Renaissance tended toward elegantly curved seat backs and upholstery fabric of sophisticated color. Italy's Poltrona Frau caught my attention with stylish designs that flaunted bright red upholstery. The offerings from the US manufacturer Irwin Seating Company were not especially impressive in regard to construction or comfort but were extremely functional.

Performance hall seating became a subject of attention for me again in 2014. That was when I undertook the design of what became the Kamaishi Civic Hall, Tetto. The project was for replacing a structure that was a victim of the Great East Japan Earthquake in 2011.

Collapsing the rear seat banks on the first level and stowing them in the back of the hall allows for shaping an 838-seat arena. The seats are of standard specifications, but they are extremely comfortable. I take that as evidence of the superiority of Japanese manufacturing.

Choosing the upholstery fabric was especially difficult. The architects of the Tokyo Bunka Kaikan

(completed in 1961, remodeled in 2014) and other prominent performance halls had elected to mix seat colors. I wanted to do likewise in Kamaishi. But budgetary constraints and the need for harmonizing with the cedar-toned interior limited my latitude in that regard. I therefore settled on black and shades of gray.

We tried several variations that consisted of different shades of warp and woof and that looked black at a distance, but each was less than fully satisfactory. I was disinclined at that point, however, to throw things open by experimenting with the addition of colored thread.

The solution, I discovered, was on what is ordinarily the reverse side of the fabric. Seemingly minor differences in weave produced subtle differences in appearance between the outer and reverse sides. I had arrived at a solution that offered a unifying tonal harmony among different shades and that was within the budget.

Selecting three fabrics and using the outer and reverse sides of each yielded six tonal variations. The result was a subdued tone overall, but the chromatic restraint seemed suitable for a venue dedicated to reconstruction and to the memory of those lost. The solution was my way of expressing support for the people of Kamaishi, literally from inside out. It resulted in seats that each embrace their occupant with sensitivity and that come together as a whole to exert a reassuring sense of collective strength.

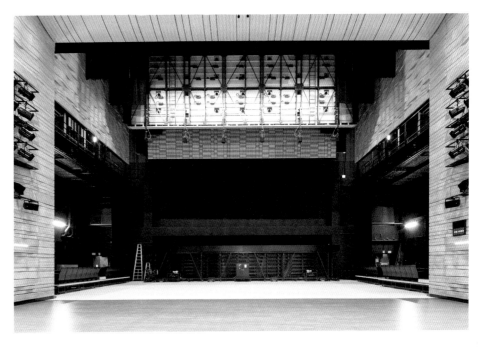

A Platform for Community Inspiration

Tamanoi Mamoru Former director, Tetto

Kamaishi Civic Hall, Tetto, appeared seven years after the Great East Japan Earthquake in fulfillment of the citizens' longing. It stands in central Kamaishi as the successor to the civic center lost to the disaster. Tetto carries the hopes and dreams of the citizenry for generating renewed vitality in the city.

The city government's reconstruction plan calls for Kamaishi to brighten the Sanriku region as a beacon of hope and smiles. That includes shaping a city center that is safe and appealing and that fulfills basic urban functions. Tetto has a diverse role to play in tackling that quest. It needs to be a platform that provides comprehensive support for initiatives intended to advance citizen welfare and enrich the community culturally. That needs to include preserving traditional culture, providing lifelong education, cultivating the human resources of tomorrow, and strengthening social bonds. All of these elements are part of Kamaishi civic culture. And Tetto's planners have equipped the facility to address all of them and thus contribute to nurturing urban symbiosis.

Tetto's architects have brought passion and imagination to the task of satisfying the expectations of the people of Kamaishi. They have achieved a facility that possesses all of the functions cited and that will thereby help citizens take pride in replicating the cultural DNA of their community and continue making their homes here. They have brought light to a city that had plunged into darkness, promoted human interchange by attracting new faces to the city, created a pleasant spot where people gather spontaneously, established a space both stimulating and comforting in eliciting the exercise of the creative instinct, and supplemented residential functions through the community hall offerings.

Those charged with administering Tetto shoulder immense responsibility. They have the job of earning the confidence of the citizenry with a facility that engenders passion. The job is one of converting bricks and mortar into friendship and camaraderie and of converting friendship and camaraderie into dreams and aspirations. It is a job to be undertaken hand in hand with the people of Kamaishi. Let us pray that the muse will continue to draw smiles to citizens' faces in Tetto's gracious lobby and in the seats of its reassuring, wood-lined halls.

Kadare (Yurihonjo City Cultural Center)

■ Location: Yurihonjo City, Akita ■ Owner: Yurihonjo City ■ Architect: Chiaki Arai Urban and Architecture Design
■ Completed: 2011 ■ Seating: Main Hall, 1,110; Gallery, 216 (Galleries 1–3 combined)

The Akita city of Yurihonjo was born of the 2005 merger of a city and seven towns. Its Yurihonjo City Cultural Center, Kadare, is a platform for educational, cultural, and social activity. Kadare serves Yurihonjo, which had a population of about 77,000 residents in 2019, with a civic hall, a planetarium, a restaurant, and an exhibition space for local products.

What first catches the eye on approaching Kadare are the multifaceted structure of exposed concrete and the oval planetarium dome. As with the Rias Hall (p. 168), the architect Arai Chiaki held workshops to secure input from the citizenry in developing the design. What emerged from the interchange was the concept of a "ship of science" for carrying youth to new perspectives and understanding.

Ideas volunteered by Yurihonjo citizens took shape in the design of the facilities inside, such as the 220,000-volume library, as well as in the building's outer configuration. They contribute to generating appeal that draws 560,000 visitors to Kadare annually.

Kadare's Main Hall, seen here, boasts a full complement of audio equipment and stage fixtures for musical and theatrical productions. The seating is of original design, which deploys the same configuration and upholstery in the stowable seats as in their fixed counterparts. Embossed ribbing in the seat backs reinforces a modernistic atmosphere in the hall.

The Main Hall is also notable for its flexible multifunctionality. Its first-level seating, for example, is stowable under the floor. Kadare's entire first floor can open to the park outside the building as a single, 130-meter-long arena. That space, including the first level of the Main Hall, is useful for festivals and other sprawling events.

The Theater as a Musical Instrument

Arai Chiaki Architect

People come not just to listen to the sounds but also to see the sights. The bustle in the foyer and inside the performance hall. The spectators and the performers. Seeing and being seen. Here arises a curious solidarity. Coming here is something more for the visitors than enjoying the concert or the play.

Each of the instruments, for example, has a distinctive shape and sound in accordance with its role. The same holds for the performance halls. Each is the result of countless hours of discussions among individuals in meetings and workshops. No ceiling or wall or seat is a ready-made product. Each is unique to its setting.

Influencing the shape of each hall is a "topophilic" regional belonging. Figuring definitively in the design of each venue is a unique background of expectations and myths. In partnership with the citizenry do the architects develop a script for the project at hand.

Rias Hall (Ofunato Civic Cultural Center and Library)
(pp. 168–171)

The fishing port of Ofunato lies on the famously ria-configured Sanriku Coast. An especially popular sight nearby is Anatoshi-iso (pass-through hole rock). That rock formation presents three holes above the water large enough for small craft to pass through. Other popular landmarks are the Goishi (igo stone) Coast, Ramboya (ruffian gorge), and Kaminari-iwa (thunder rock).

Rias Hall is of a geometry rendered possible by technological advances in architectural modeling. Guests pass through the evocative setting of Ofunato and into a cave-like interior. There, they take their places and lean into seat backs that trace wavy profiles along each row. The stuff of legend is in the air.

Kadare (Yurihonjo City Cultural Center)
(pp. 194–197)

Yurihonjo City has a long tradition of emphasizing science education. It has had a planetarium- and library-equipped civic center, for instance, since the 1980s. Kadare carries on that tradition as the home for the library and planetarium, which share the facility with a modern performance hall. The building's main unit is cylindrical, 12.5 meters wide and 85.0 meters long. It

has the look of a spaceship, which stimulates young imaginations. Three-dimensional modeling based on the finite element method was indispensable in designing the building's complex contours.

Niigata City Konan Ward Cultural Center
(pp. 200–201)

The Kameda district of Niigata City's Konan Ward is famous for delectable rice and fine sake. Planting the rice entailed, until mechanization transformed the work in the late 1940s, walking waist-deep in flooded paddies. The color of the ears of rice displays gradations through the summer. Neither gales nor rain fell the stalks. Manifest even in fragrance, ever changing, is the life force of the plants.

Theater, Civic Hall, Library, and Historical Museum come together at the Niigata City Konan Ward Cultural Center in a unified assertion of light and sound. In the Theater, 7,000 holes in the white ceiling shape the acoustics and, with LEDs, the illumination in the hall. The pattern on the upholstery fabric emulates the stripes of the locally produced Kamedajima cotton fabric and evokes the scene of rice plants growing.

Akiha Ward Cultural Center
(pp. 202–203)

Embedded light sources. Ceiling windows that admit natural lumens from outside. Curving columns. Twisting walls. Awaiting sojourners in this cavernous environment: discovery. Event-goers sit back in autumn-leaf seats and give themselves over to the embrace of the enigmatically contoured concrete environs. They have entered a world wholly unexpected in the Niitsu district of Niigata City's Akiha Ward.

Here in the Akiha Ward Cultural Center careful acoustical engineering has gone into the architectural design. Most of the wall and ceiling elements perform a structural function and cannot be moved. So acoustical considerations needed to receive careful attention, starting in the earliest stages of the design process. That attention has paid off handsomely. The hall has earned especially high regard for its acoustical performance in the bass range.

Niigata City Konan Ward Cultural Center

■ Location: Niigata City, Niigata ■ Owner: Niigata City ■ Architect: Chiaki Arai Urban and Architecture Design
■ Completed: 2012 ■ Seating: 399 (Theater)

When Niigata City adopted a plan for a new cultural center, it opted to move its civic hall, library, and historical museum to the new building. Vertical ribs on the exposed concrete suggest the stalks of the rice that grows abundantly in Niigata and the stripes of the locally produced Kamedajima cotton fabric.

The energizing light of life is the theme for the entire Niigata City Konan Ward Cultural Center. In the Theater, light twinkles from LEDs scattered across the ceiling. It produces striking optical effects on the seating's green upholstery, the color and pattern of which are a reference to Niigata's rice-growing countryside. Movable acoustic panels allow for extending the stage to a depth of about 11 meters. The stage can then accommodate a full orchestra, which is remarkable for a hall that seats only 399 people. Part of the stage supports additional seating for performances of traditional Japanese music and for talks and movie screenings. Each of the four facilities—Theater, Civic Hall, Library, and Historical Museum—occupies a zone delineated by corridors. That begets a shared purposefulness for the users of each facility.

Akiha Ward Cultural Center

■ Location: Niigata City, Niigata ■ Owner: Niigata City ■ Architect: Chiaki Arai Urban and Architecture Design
■ Completed: 2013 ■ Seating: 496

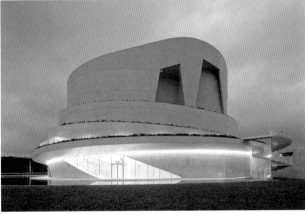

Standing near Niigata's Niitsu Hill, the Akiha Ward Cultural Center reflects the bluff's topography in its architecture. As a platform for nurturing community spirit, the center also reflects the spiritual respite afforded by the hillside greenery. Meeting rooms, practice rooms, and the lobby line the hallway and interconnect in the manner of the nearby hiking trails. The rounded walls and ceiling of the cave-like hall convey high-quality sound. Aluminum vanes in the windows enhance the acoustics further and filter light in the manner of forest trees.

Festival Hall

- Location: Osaka City, Osaka ■ Owner: Asahi Shimbun Company ■ Architect: Nikken Sekkei
- Completed: 2013 ■ Seating: 2,700

Standing on the former site of an illustrious predecessor, Festival Hall has inherited a weighty heritage. The original hall, opened in 1958, was Japan's premier concert hall for 50 years, with its 2,700-seat capacity and its sublime acoustics. A redevelopment project included demolishing the office building that housed the first-generation Festival Hall in 2008 and replacing it with the 39-story Nakanoshima Festival Tower. The new building, which opened in 2013, houses Festival Hall on its second to seventh floors.

Festival Hall inherits its predecessor's 2,700-seat capacity, broad stage, and proximity to the stage for all the seats in the house. It has supplemented those virtues, meanwhile, with upgraded stage fixtures, including a tall and deep fly tower. The reborn Festival Hall thus supports an expanded range of artistic expression.

Honoring and Building on Tradition
Kabuto Katsuyuki   Nikken Sekkei

Festival Hall opened in 2013 as the successor to a hall famed for acoustics akin to sound pouring down from heaven. We sought in the stage equipment and in the acoustical engineering to honor the tradition of the hall's illustrious predecessor while advancing and building on that tradition.

Guests arrive at the entrance hall via a red-carpeted staircase. The foyer is a three-level, brick-walled atrium. Its lighting, suggestive of a starry sky, sets the mood for the performance about to begin inside the concert hall.

The new hall has the same 2,700-seat capacity as its predecessor but deploys the seating over three levels instead of the first-generation hall's two levels. We have promoted audience-performer engagement, meanwhile, by shortening the distance between the stage and the rearmost seats by two meters.

Seating comfort has benefited from increasing the width of the seats by five centimeters and the depth by four centimeters. We worked with a series of mock-ups to optimize the comfort and styling of the seating. The seating inherited the cherrywood fittings and moquette upholstery of that in the earlier hall. Handrails built into the seating on the second and third levels enhance safety, especially for the elderly.

Festival Hall has won praise as a concert hall from musicians and listeners who knew well the fabulous acoustics of its predecessor. It is itself something of a musical instrument. Wood surfacing is on view throughout the hall. The flooring under the audience seating is rosewood, the same material used in violins, guitars, and clarinets.

Ueda Santomyuze

- Location: Ueda City, Nagano ■ Owner: Ueda City ■ Architects: Yanagisawa Takahiko + TAK Architects Inc., Azusa Sekkei
- Completed: 2014 ■ Seating: Theater, 1,530; Hall, 320

Standing alongside the Chikumagawa river, Ueda Santomyuze houses the Ueda Performing Arts and Cultural Center and the Ueda City Museum of Art. The center and the museum, along with ancillary facilities, lie around an expansive lawn. Visitors enjoy a spectacular view of Ueda's mountain scenery from the walkway that links the facilities.

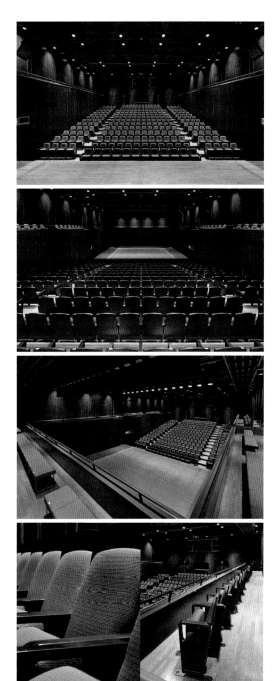

The Theater (pp. 208 and 210–211) can accommodate large-scale orchestral performances and theatrical and ballet productions. Its compact design positions the entire audience within 31 meters of the stage. That makes the theater an effective venue, too, for traditional genres of Japanese performance arts and for talks.

Harmonizing with the wood floor and the wood-paneled walls are the subdued, black tones of the seat fittings. Horizonal rows of tiny triangles in the green upholstery fabric invite association with the mountainous landscape around Ueda. The three-colored weave of the fabric in the first-level seats and in the second-level balcony seats is eye-catching, as is the triangular opening under each armrest.

A year-round program of music, drama, dance, and talks unfolds in the Hall (above, right, p. 211). The venue supplements 288 first-level seats with 32 second-level balcony seats. Here, the seating complements the natural wood interior and heightens audience engagement with dark red upholstery. The second-level seating is a combination of fixed seat banks above the first-level seating and movable bench seats toward and above the stage. Its bench seats sometimes become part of the staging for works that require high positioning for performers.

Westa Kawagoe

■ Location: Kawagoe City, Saitama ■ Owners: Kawagoe City and Saitama Prefecture ■ Architect: AXS Satow
■ Completed: 2015 ■ Seating: Main Hall, 1,712; Multipurpose Hall, 780 (theater configuration)

Sharing Westa Kawagoe, on the west side of Kawagoe's main passenger train station, are municipal and prefectural facilities. They include a passport center, a childcare support center, performance and multipurpose halls, conference rooms, and study and activity rooms for lifelong education. The Main Hall, equipped with state-of-the-art stage equipment, lighting, and audio, hosts classical music, opera, drama, ballet, and traditional Japanese performance genres, including Noh, Kyogen, Kabuki, and dance. Optimizing the angles of the three tiers of seating has helped ensure that every guest can absorb the performances fully.

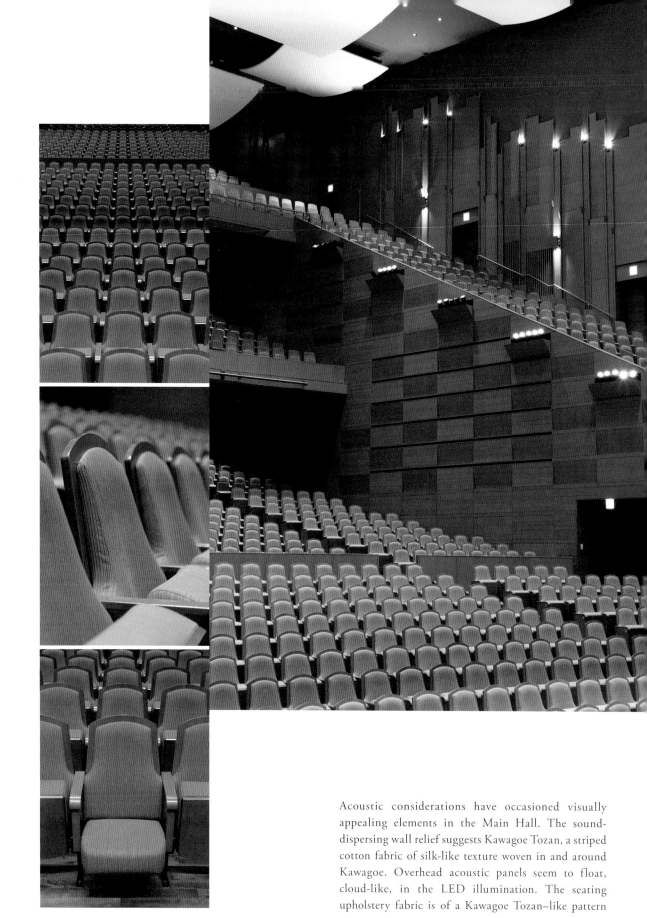

Acoustic considerations have occasioned visually appealing elements in the Main Hall. The sound-dispersing wall relief suggests Kawagoe Tozan, a striped cotton fabric of silk-like texture woven in and around Kawagoe. Overhead acoustic panels seem to float, cloud-like, in the LED illumination. The seating upholstery fabric is of a Kawagoe Tozan–like pattern

that resonates with the geometrical patterns on the walls. Red threads in the weave symbolize the festive character of stage performances, and the vertical stripes represent the Kawagoe cityscape. The form-fitting cushioning of the seat backs and the weight-dispersing upholstery of the chair seats helps ensure comfort through even long performances.

Küste

■ Location: Katsuura City, Chiba ■ Owner: Katsuura City ■ Architect: Yamashita Sekkei, Inc.
■ Completed: 2014 ■ Seating: 826

Katsuura has long thrived as a fishing port, and it has supplemented its vitality in recent years with popular tourist attractions, such as Katsuura Undersea Park. The city has further strengthened its appeal for residents and visitors alike with the cultural exchange center Küste. Distinguishing the Küste building (bottom, p. 218) is a two-tiered symbolism: glass walls on the first floor, signifying the sea, and louvered facings of twisting bricks on the second floor, signifying sandy beaches.

Küste's twisting brick louvers are more than a design artifice. They fulfill an important function in filtering the intense sunshine that beats down on Katsuura's position on Chiba's Boso Peninsula. Inside the hall, brick helixes perform a valuable function in enhancing the acoustics.

LEDs provide all of the illumination for the stage and for the seating, which reduces energy consumption and maintenance costs immensely. The first-floor seating is movable and stowable (top, p. 217), allowing for transforming the hall into an open arena (bottom, p. 219). Thus can the hall accommodate diverse events and even serve, as necessary, as an emergency-response center.

Kure Kizuna Hall

■ Location: Kure City, Hiroshima ■ Owner: Kuro City ■ Architect. Daiken Sekkei, Inc.
■ Completed: 2016 ■ Seating: 581

Kure City replaced its aging municipal headquarters complex with, on the same site, a city hall building and a civic center, Kure Kizuna Hall. *Kizuna* means "ties," as in "the ties that bind." Connecting the city hall and Kure Kizuna Hall is the airy Civic Mall (top, left, p. 221), which provides an organic linkage between administrative and cultural functions.

Movable acoustic panels optimize the proscenium-arch Kure Kizuna Hall for musical concerts, and the hall renders service, too, as a venue for ceremonies and talks. Also movable are the seating blocks. Hall staff can reposition the blocks, which contain electric drive systems, with remote control units. They can even stow the seating blocks behind sliding walls. The hall then becomes an approximately 500-square-meter arena that opens directly onto the Civic Mall (bottom, right, p. 222). When torrential rains struck the region in 2018, the hall served as an emergency-response base.

The seat backs narrow toward the top and present rounded profiles suggestive of candle flames. Reinforcing the flame imagery is the chromatic gradation in the upholstery fabric. Stowage for the movable seating blocks is on the stage side and foyer side of the hall.

Big Roof Takizawa

■ Location: Takizawa City, Iwate　■ Owner: Takizawa City　■ Architect: Tohoku Branch, Mitsubishi Jisho Sekkei Inc.
■ Completed: 2016　■ Seating: Large Hall, 462; Small Hall, 144

C 大ホール 2扉

The sweeping roof replicates the gently sloping profile of the mountain Iwatesan, visible from a central courtyard of Big Roof Takizawa. Each of the facilities in the complex is accessible from the courtyard, which is thus a plaza for personal interaction.

Scattered through the mainly black seating in the dark-toned Large Hall are a few seats upholstered in red, green, or blue. The daubs of color pay homage to a local tradition designated an intangible cultural property by the Japanese government. That is an annual festival that sees local equestrians ride 14 kilometers on gaudily costumed horses.

At maximum capacity, the seating is a combination of three movable blocks at the back of the hall and of stackable seats arrayed in the front. Air casters make moving the seat blocks easy. The flexibility accommodates a vast range of performances and even indoor sports events.

Namiki Square

■ Location: Fukuoka City, Fukuoka ■ Owner: Fukuoka City ■ Architect: Yamashita Sekkei, Inc.
■ Completed: 2016 ■ Seating: 800 (Namiki Hall)

Namiki Hall (pp. 228–230) shares the Namiki Square cultural complex with a library, rehearsal halls, and other complementary facilities, including a day care room and a bakery. The name *namiki* means "tree row," and walking to Namiki Square from the nearby Chihaya (passenger train) Station takes the visitor across a tree-lined boulevard and past rows of trees on the grounds of the complex.

Constructing Namiki Square with a minimum of walls and beams has produced a continuum between outside and inside. Passersby can see what's going on inside the building, and the people inside retain a visual connection with the cityscape outside. Namiki Hall and the other Namiki Square facilities are readily visible from the atrium at the entrance.

Upper-level seats line the Namiki Hall walls in fixtures that have the look of hanging planters and that wrap all the way around the rear of the stage. The upholstery fabric and wood fittings of the seating are black, in keeping with the chic color scheme of the hall interior, and the contrasting white numbering on the seat backs offers the dual advantages of easy legibility and stylish design.

Cominess (Shirakawa Performing Arts Theatre)

■ Location: Shirakawa City, Fukushima ■ Owner: Shirakawa City ■ Architect: Nihon Sekkei
■ Completed: 2016 ■ Seating: Big Hall, 1,104; Small Hall, 321

Shirakawa City, where the Great East Japan Earthquake wrought severe damage, erected Cominess five years after the quake as a symbol of revitalization. The building is a platform for measures to stimulate community vitality through cultural activities. It is an unassuming presence on the cityscape and harmonizes with the historical setting, including the nearby Kominejo castle. Kagigata Mall stretches through Cominess between the east and west entrances and past the Big Hall, Small Hall, dressing rooms, rehearsal rooms, and a courtyard.

Cominess's proscenium-arch Big Hall (pp. 232–234) is primarily for musical performances and accommodates a diversity of musical genres. The red of the seating upholstery alludes to the Rakuou weeping cherry tree that stands in Shirakawa and is reportedly 200 years old. Horizontal pink stripes across the fabric resonate with the ribbed wall panels. Sixteen cranes soar across the curtain, emphasizing the Cominess theme of revitalization. They are the work of Imai Shusen, a noted *nihonga* artist from Shirakawa.

Removable seating facilitates adapting Cominess's Small Hall (above, p. 235) to different needs in supporting community activities. The top row of the seating can connect on left and right to the balcony-seat level, which presents the solidity of permanent seating. A natural wood curtain conceals the seating when it is folded away out of use. The white, gray, and black of the seating upholstery and fittings are a reference to Kominejo castle. As in the Big Hall, the striped weave resonates with the ribbed wall panels in the hall.

Tsuruoka Art Culture Terrace

■ Location: Tsuruoka City, Yamagata ■ Owner: Tsuruoka City ■ Architects: SANAA, Niibo Kenchiku Sekkei, Ishikawa Sekkei Office
■ Completed: 2017 ■ Seating: Large Hall, 1,120; Small Hall, 180

The Tsuruoka Art Culture Terrace stands in a historic corner of Tsuruoka City. Just steps away is the Chidokan, a school established in 1805 by the clan that controlled the region around Tsuruoka. Nearby are rolling mountains, whose ridgelines have influenced the sweeping rooflines on the modernistic architecture of the Tsuruoka Art Culture Terrace.

A passageway winds through the building, past the Small Hall, dressing rooms, rehearsal rooms, meeting rooms, a day care room, and other ancillary rooms. Along the passageway are sofas and chairs designed by SANAA, the lead architectural firm in the Tsuruoka Art Culture Terrace project.

Adopting a vineyard-style layout in the Large Hall has engendered an immediacy between the audience and the performers. Projecting balcony seats over the rear seating on the first level has minimized the distance from the stage for everyone.

In accordance with the architects' instructions, straight-line configurations prevail in the seat backs, the chair seats, and the legs. A handcrafted angularity for the seat backs and armrests emphasizes the throwback character of the seating design. And light-toned fabric covering for the seating upholstery brightens the mood overall.

Mt. Fuji World Heritage Centre, Shizuoka

■ Location: Fujinomiya City, Shizuoka ■ Owner: Shizuoka Prefecture Architect: Shigeru Ban Architects
■ Completed: 2017 ■ Seating: 74 (Audio-Visual Theater)

In June 2013, the United Nations Educational, Scientific and Cultural Organization (UNESCO), inscribed Japan's tallest peak on the list of world heritage sites as "Fujisan, sacred place and source of artistic inspiration." The Mt. Fuji World Heritage Centre, Shizuoka, opened in 2017, is a platform for supporting the study of the mountain's role in Japanese culture and religion.

Architect Ban Shigeru's inverted, cypress-clad cone casts a reflection in the reflecting pool that mirrors Fujisan's profile. The water is from spring water drawn from the slopes of Fujisan and serves as coolant in the center's air-conditioning system. Its multiple usage symbolizes the water cycle.

Visitors ascend and descend a spiral slope between levels one to five of the center to view the displays in the center. Images cast on the wall of the routes up Fujisan give the experience of actually traversing the mountain. A look at the real Fujisan is the reward for reaching the top floor of the inverted cone (pp. 240–241).

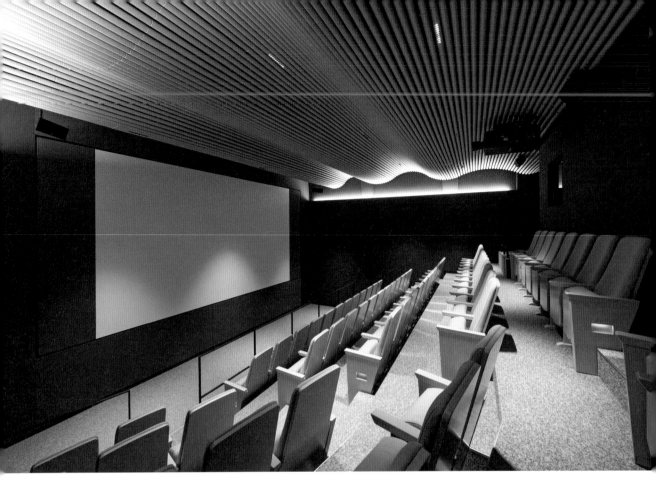

Presentations in the second-floor Audio-Visual Theater (p. 242) offer an archival record of activity on the mountain paths. A wavy ceiling of paper tubes lends a curious atmosphere to the space. The seating, of unpainted wood and beige upholstery, is of minimalist configuration.

Nippon Seinen-kan Hall

■ Location: Shinjuku Ward, Tokyo ■ Owner: Nippon-Seinenkan ■ Architect: Kume Sekkei Co., Ltd.
■ Completed: 2017 ■ Seating: 1,249

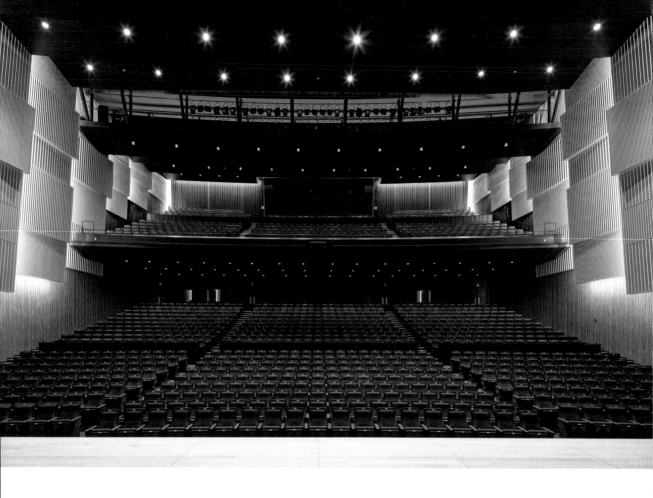

Promoting cultural and sporting activity and international exchange among young people is the express purpose of the Nippon Seinen-kan Hall. Japan's successful bid to hold the 2020 Olympic and Paralympic Games occasioned the rebuilding of the hall, which is near the new National Stadium. This is the third-generation Nippon Seinen-kan Hall. It stands 80 meters south of the site of its predecessor, which was built in 1925 and rebuilt in 1979.

The Nippon Seinen-kan Hall occupies the first to fourth floors of the 16-story building. On the fifth to eighth floors are offices, and a hotel occupies the floors above. The hall inherits the basic shape and the vertically grained wood paneling of the second-generation hall. Filtered lighting sets an aesthetic tone.

In the seating, wood fittings of brown and dark gray and upholstery fabric of chromatically textured green evoke the parkland verdure around the Nippon Seinen-kan Hall. Varying the tone of green upholstery across three levels—darker at the front of the hall, lighter toward the rear—amplifies the sense of depth. The seat backs and the chair seats narrow outward, lending a sharp profile to the seating. A compact configuration for the seats maximizes the breadth of the aisles.

Danjuro (Echigo Tsumari Auditorium)

■ Location: Tokamachi City, Niigata ■ Owner: Tokamachi City ■ Architects: Azusa Sekkei, Tsukada Sekkei
■ Completed: 2017 ■ Seating: 708

Several facilities came together under the common roof of the Tokamachi Central Community Center, including the impressive concert hall: Echigo Tsumari Auditorium, Danjuro. Building Danjuro was an initiative for promoting interaction among members of the community through cultural and social undertakings.

The proscenium-arch hall evokes the ancient pottery (3500–2500 BCE) embellished with flame-like ornamentation that has been unearthed in Tokamachi.

The hall's stage curtain presents different colors and patterns when viewed from different angles, like the glimmering surface of the nearby Shinanogawa river and the dancing flames on Tokamachi's ancient pottery. The hall, though mainly for musical performances, also accommodates theatrical performances and talks. It has, for example, a *hanamichi* walkway that can be installed for Kabuki and other traditional performance genres.

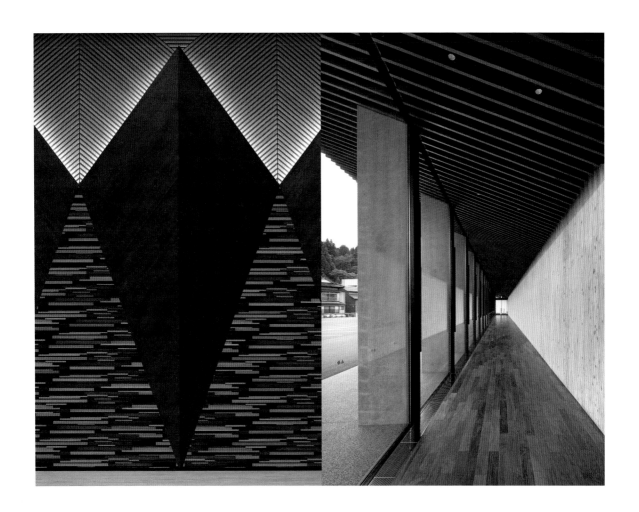

Danjuro cuts a sharp profile with its steep roof, which captures and casts a varying pattern of shadows through the day and through the changing seasons. Stretching alongside the auditorium is the 110-meter Gangi Gallery (above, right, p. 251). Fitted with overhead louvers of Niigata cedar, it suggests the region's extended *gangi* eaves for keeping sidewalks clear of snow. Tokamachi has long been famous for the kimono made there, and a rooftop overlay of varicolored silk woven by local artists produces stunning visual effects come evening in the Gangi Gallery.

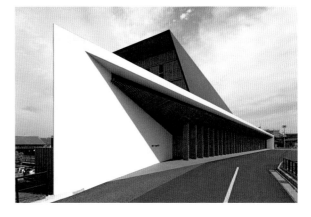

hitaru (Sapporo Cultural Arts Theater)

■ Location: Sapporo City, Hokkaido ■ Owner: Sapporo City ■ Architects: Nikken Sekkei, Hokkaido Nikken Sekkei
■ Completed: 2018 ■ Seating: Theater, 2,302; Creative Studio, 400

The Sapporo Community Plaza took shape as part of Sapporo Sosei Square, which arose through a massive redevelopment project. It has brought a new touch to Sapporo lifestyles, evidenced by the library users bearing coffee from the first-floor café. The center's premier attraction is the Sapporo Cultural Arts Theater, hitaru (pp. 252–255 and 258). That venue is a large hall fitted with multiple stages for rotating sets smoothly and quickly to support full-scale operas, ballets, and musicals.

On view in the Theater is a European flair. Red upholstery adorns the seating amid the wood-paneled walls. Three levels of balconies wrap around the proscenium-arch stage. The first-level seats fairly absorb their occupants, whereas the balcony seat backs are each of an optimized angle for listening and viewing. A commitment to optimizing the experience of appreciating performance art is manifest in the organic curvature of the first-level seating.

White birch from Hokkaido renders service in the wood fittings, including in the straight seat backs and the curved armrests. Including blue, green, and yellow thread in the weave of the upholstery fabric has resulted in a finish that changes with the angle and intensity of the incident light.

In the Creative Studio (p. 256), movable seating offers a choice of layouts. The space switches easily between a flat arena and a small auditorium equipped with stepped seating.

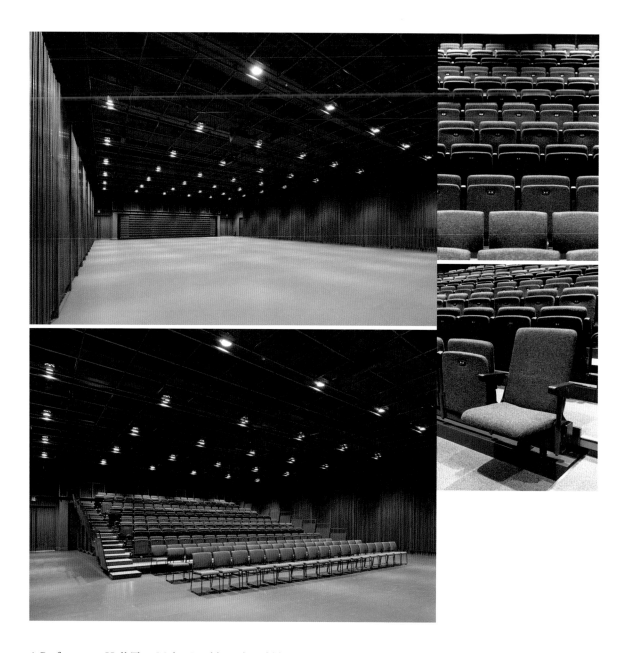

A Performance Hall That Makes Visible and Audible Happen

Nakagawa Yosuke Architect, Hokkaido Nikken Sekkei Co., Ltd.

Sapporo Sosei Square is a multiuse complex developed by public- and private-sector participants in Sapporo's city center. It comprises a 29-story office building and the 9-story Sapporo Community Plaza, which houses hitaru on its fifth to ninth floors, the Sapporo Cultural Arts Community Center (SCARTS) on its first to fourth floors, the Sapporo Municipal Library and Information Center on its first and second floors, and a café and restaurant on its first floor.

Among the tenants in the office building are a television broadcaster and the Hokkaido branch of a national newspaper. The builders outfitted Sapporo Sosei Square with a district cooling and heating plant,

an indoor parking garage, and a public parking facility for bicycles.

Positioning the Sapporo Community Plaza as a cultural beacon depended on securing a robust flow of visitors on a daily basis. We on the design team therefore placed the facilities subject to continuing visitor traffic on the readily accessible lower floors and the hitaru theater on the uppermost floors. SCARTS Mall, an atrium, provides vertical, three-dimensional linkage among the different facilities in the Sapporo Community Plaza. The air-conditioned space is especially welcome as a warm sanctuary during snowy Sapporo's winter months.

Hitaru has succeeded Nitori Culture Hall as Sapporo's only large performance facility. It is an ideal venue for opera and ballet productions and for orchestral concerts. The design maximizes visibility even from the balcony seats. A segmented configuration for the balconies optimizes the seating angle in each balcony from the standpoint of visibility. The three levels of balconies (p. 258) veritably embrace the stage, furnishing occupants with a richly palpable experience of the performances.

Measures for achieving acoustical clarity and resonance included repeated testing with a one-tenth-scale model. The results of that testing furnished a basis for acoustically optimizing the positioning of the sound-reflecting ceiling panels and the contouring of the walls and balconies.

Allusions to Hokkaido's natural environment abound. Wood surfacing prevails in the interior. The front panels on the balconies trace an undulating line in the manner of a rolling landscape. And indirect lighting illuminates the walls in a way that suggests light filtered by trees in a forest.

Hitaru exemplifies the importance of making visible and audible happen in a performance hall. Superb visibility combines with excellent audibility to bring the audience and performers together. Here is a prize venue for experiencing performance arts.

The Venues in Brief*

*Location, owner(s), architect(s), date of completion, date of major remodeling (if applicable), and maximum seating capacity (including fixed seating, movable seating, removable seating, and wheelchair seating space)

Chapter 1

pp. 200–201
Niigata City Konan Ward Cultural Center
Location   Niigata City, Niigata
Owner   Niigata City
Architect   Chiaki Arai Urban and Architecture Design
Completed   2012
Seating   399 (Theater)

pp. 202–203
Akiba Ward Cultural Center
Location   Niigata City, Niigata
Owner   Niigata City
Architect   Chiaki Arai Urban and Architecture Design
Completed   2013
Seating   496

pp. 204–207
Festival Hall
Location   Osaka City, Osaka
Owner   Asahi Shimbun Company
Architect   Nikken Sekkei Ltd.
Completed   2013
Seating   2,700

pp. 208–211
Ueda Santomyuze
Location   Ueda City, Nagano
Owner   Ueda City
Architects   Yanagisawa Takahiko + TAK Architects Inc., Azusa Sekkei
Completed   2014
Seating   Theater, 1,530; Hall, 320

pp. 212–215
Westa Kawagoe
Location   Kawagoe City, Saitama
Owners   Kawagoe City and Saitama Prefecture
Architect   AXS Satow
Completed   2015
Seating   Main Hall, 1,712;
           Multipurpose Hall, 780 (theater configuration)

pp. 216–219
Küste
Location   Katsuura City, Chiba
Owner   Katsuura City
Architect   Yamashita Sekkei, Inc.
Completed   2014
Seating   826

pp. 220–223
Kure Kizuna Hall
Location   Kure City, Hiroshima
Owner   Kure City
Architect   Daiken Sekkei, Inc.
Completed   2016
Seating   581

pp. 224–227
Big Roof Takizawa
Location   Takizawa City, Iwate
Owner   Takizawa City
Architect   Tohoku Branch, Mitsubishi Jisho Sekkei Inc.
Completed   2016
Seating   Large Hall, 462; Small Hall, 144

pp. 228–231
Namiki Square
Location   Fukuoka City, Fukuoka
Owner   Fukuoka City
Architect   Yamashita Sekkei, Inc.
Completed   2016
Seating   800 (Namiki Hall)

pp. 232–235
Cominess (Shirakawa Performing Arts Theatre)
Location   Shirakawa City, Fukushima
Owner   Shirakawa City
Architect   Nihon Sekkei
Completed   2016
Seating   Big Hall, 1,104; Small Hall, 321

pp. 236–239
Tsuruoka Art Culture Terrace
Location   Tsuruoka City, Yamagata
Owner   Tsuruoka City
Architects   SANAA, Niibo Kenchiku Sekkei, Ishikawa Sekkei Office
Completed   2017
Seating   Large Hall, 1,120; Small Hall, 180

pp. 240–243
Mt. Fuji World Heritage Centre, Shizuoka
Location   Fujinomiya City, Shizuoka
Owner   Shizuoka Prefecture
Architect   Shigeru Ban Architects
Completed   2017
Seating   74 (Audio-Visual Theater)

pp. 244–247
Nippon Seinen-kan Hall
Location   Shinjuku Ward, Tokyo
Owner   Nippon-Seinenkan
Architect   Kume Sekkei Co., Ltd.
Completed   2017
Seating   1,249

pp. 248–251
Danjuro (Echigo Tsumari Auditorium)
Location   Tokamachi City, Niigata
Owner   Tokamachi City
Architects   Azusa Sekkei, Tsukada Sekkei
Completed   2017
Seating   708

pp. 252–258
hitaru (Sapporo Cultural Arts Theater)
Location   Sapporo City, Hokkaido
Owner   Sapporo City
Architects   Nikken Sekkei Ltd.; Hokkaido Nikken Sekkei
Completed   2018
Seating   Theater, 2,302; Creative Studio, 400

Photo Credits

Photographers

Fumio Araki
pp. 20–26; p. 27, top; p. 36; pp. 38–39; p. 40, top;
p. 41, top; pp. 42–45; p. 58; pp. 60–61;
pp. 208–211; pp. 248–251

Katsuhiko Murata
pp. 28–31; pp. 54–57; pp. 74–75; pp. 76–77;
pp. 78–81; pp. 82–84; p. 85, bottom left and right;
pp. 86–89; pp. 104–107; pp. 112–117;
p. 144, bottom; pp. 146–148; pp. 166–167;
pp. 172–175; pp. 188–192;
p. 200, bottom left and right; pp. 204–206;
p. 207, top, bottom left and right; pp. 212–214;
p. 215, middle, bottom; pp. 216–219; pp. 224–227;
pp. 228–231; pp. 232–235; p. 236;
p. 237, top, bottom; pp. 238–239; p. 242;
p. 243, bottom left and right; pp. 244–247;
pp. 252–254; p. 255, top (three); p. 256;
p. 257, top; p. 258

Tokuaki Takimoto
pp. 32–35; p. 68, bottom; pp. 96; p. 97, top; p. 108;
p. 109, top; pp. 110–111; pp. 126–128; pp. 130–131;
pp. 132–135; pp. 142–143; p. 144, top; p. 145;
pp. 158–160; p. 161, top; p. 162, top; pp. 163–164;
p. 165, top; pp. 182–184

Shigeo Ogawa
p. 37, bottom; p. 40, bottom; p. 41, bottom;
pp. 64–66; p. 67, top, middle; p. 68, top

Shigeru Ohno
p. 47, top; pp. 70–73; pp. 140–141; pp. 150–152;
p. 153, top right, middle, bottom left and right;
pp. 154–155; p. 156; p. 157, top, bottom left;
p. 178, bottom; p. 179, bottom; p. 194;
p. 195, bottom left

Kazunari Satoh
pp. 48–53; pp. 98–103; pp. 136–139; pp. 176–177;
p. 178, middle; pp. 220–223

Katsuhisa Kida
p. 97, bottom right

Satoshi Asakawa
p. 129

Tsuyoshi Taira
p. 157, bottom right

Sergio Pirrone
pp. 168–170; p. 171, middle center and right, bottom;
p. 195, top left and right, middle, bottom right; p. 198;
p. 200, top; p. 201; pp. 202–203

Taisuke Ogawa
p. 171, top, middle left; pp. 196–197

Yasutake Kondo
p. 178, top; p. 179, top

Atsushi Okuyama
p. 193

Hiroyuki Hirai
pp. 240–241; p. 243, top

Takehiro Kawamura, Creative Eyes
p. 255, bottom; p. 257, bottom

Kotobuki Seating Archive
p. 46, top; p. 91; p. 92, top, bottom right; pp. 120–
122; p.123, bottom; p. 125

Other sources

Tokyo Bunka Kaikan
p. 27, bottom

Japan Arts Council
p. 46, bottom

National Noh Theatre
p. 47, bottom

Suntory Hall
pp. 54–57

NHK Symphony Orchestra, Tokyo
pp. 54–57

Tokyu Corporation
p. 59, top

Saitama Arts Theater
pp. 64–67; p. 68, top; p. 69

Yokosuka Arts Theatre
p. 85, top

Sinphonia Iwakuni
p. 90; p. 93

Niigata City Art & Culture Promotion Foundation
pp. 94–95

Itsuko Hasegawa Atelier
p. 97, bottom

Yokohama Minato Mirai Hall
p. 109, bottom

Ala (Kani Public Arts Center)
p. 123, top

Matsumoto Performing Arts Centre
p. 153, top left

Hyogo Performing Arts Center
p. 161, bottom

MJ Hall (Miyakonojo General Cultural Hall)
p. 162, bottom; p. 165, bottom

Naito Architect and Associates
pp. 180–181; p. 185

Asahi Shimbun Company
p. 207, bottom middle

Westa Kawagoe
p. 215, top

SANAA©
p. 237, middle

翻訳　ミラー和空
校閲　ハワード・ブラント

Translation by Waku Miller
Editing by Howard Brandt

英語版

劇場建築とイス
客席から見た小宇宙 1911–2018

Theaters and Their Seating in Japan
Architectural gems from 1911 to 2018

2020年10月8日　初版第一刷発行

Date of first publication: October 8, 2020

企画・監修　コトブキシーティング株式会社アーカイブ室
〒101-0062 東京都千代田区神田駿河台1-2-1
Tel. 03-5280-5399　Fax. 03-5280-5776
http://kotobuki-seating.co.jp

Kotobuki Seating Archive
1-2-1 Kanda Surugadai, Chiyoda-ku, Tokyo 101-0062, Japan
Tel. 03-5280-5399　Fax. 03-5280-5776
http://kotobuki-seating.co.jp

発行人　藤元由記子
発行所　株式会社ブックエンド
〒101-0021 東京都千代田区外神田6丁目11-14
アーツ千代田3331
Tel. 03-6806-0458　Fax. 03-6806-0459
http://bookend.co.jp

Bookend Co., Ltd.
3331Arts Chiyoda, 6-11-14 Sotokanda, Chiyoda-ku, Tokyo
101-0021, Japan
Tel. 03-6806-0458　Fax. 03-6806-0459
http://bookend.co.jp

ブックデザイン　折原 滋（O design）
印刷・製本　日本写真印刷コミュニケーションズ株式会社

Book Design by Shigeru Orihara
Printing and binding by Nissha Printing Communications, Inc.

Printed in Japan
ISBN978-4-907083-63-2
© 2020 Kotobuki Seating Co., Ltd.